REGENTS CONTINENTAL DRAMA SERIES

General Editor: John Loftis

RODOGUNE

PIERRE CORNEILLE

Rodogune

The French Text with a Facing English Translation

Translated and Edited by

WILLIAM G. CLUBB

UNIVERSITY OF NEBRASKA PRESS · LINCOLN

CONTENTS

Regents Continental Drama Series   vii

Introduction   ix

RODOGUNE

    French Text   2

    English Translation   3

Notes   122

Appendix: A Note on the Use of Historical Sources in *Rodogune* and a Chronology of the Kings of Syria from 150 to 65 B.C.   127

REGENTS CONTINENTAL DRAMA SERIES

The Regents Continental Drama Series will provide editions of a group of plays chosen from the periods of highest achievement in the national dramas of Western Europe. Intended to make the plays more readily accessible to English and American students, the editions will include on facing pages the text in the original language and a translation—ordinarily a prose translation, as literal as is consistent with idiomatic English. The introduction will supply information on the date of the play, its place in the author's career, its stage history, its textual history, its sources, as well as a critical interpretation. Explanatory notes are directed to the needs of mature students who are not specialists in the Continental literatures. Textual notes are provided only in instances of unusual interest. Spelling and punctuation are modernized along consciously conservative lines.

The editor and publisher have planned the series with attention to the international quality of European drama, the shared patterns of development evident in plays produced in different countries and in different centuries. It is their hope that the series will aid in the comparative study of European drama—too often frustrated because only a few men can have the linguistic skills required to read several languages without the assistance of translations.

JOHN LOFTIS

Stanford University

INTRODUCTION

DATE AND BIOGRAPHY

With the tragedy of *Rodogune, Princesse des Parthes*, first performed late in 1644 or early in 1645,[1] Pierre Corneille reached the acme of his life and career. Not long before, he had married, and two of his eventual seven children were already born. Soon after, he was elected to the Académie Française, a more than welcome honor, in view of that body's notorious judgment on *Le Cid* in 1638. But also in his thirty-eighth year Corneille completed the last of the plays for which continental Europe would for more than a century call him its greatest tragic poet. After *Rodogune* there is nothing to equal it or the best of the preceding decade. To be sure, more than one of the following plays was briefly as successful in the theater as *Cinna*, for example, but by 1674 there was general agreement that Boileau's quasi-official condemnation of Corneille's later work, though prejudiced, was not entirely unjust.[2] Only *Nicomède* has survived in repertory and in criticism.

In the first part of a dramatic career that began sometime between 1625 and 1629, Corneille limited himself for the most part to experiments with comic and mixed genres that had not quite emerged fully in France,[3] the most characteristic being a tragi-comedy, *Clitandre*, a serious comedy, *La Suivante* (all his comedies are relatively serious, with wit and sophistication in the place of low farce), and a work of bold generic conflation, *L'Illusion comique*—a

---

1. Louis Herland, *Corneille par lui-même* (Paris, 1956), p. 21. Jacques Scherer, in his critical edition of *Rodogune* (Paris, 1946), Antoine Adam, in *Histoire de la littérature française au XVIIe siècle*, vol. 2 (Paris, 1954), and Henry Carrington Lancaster, in *A History of French Dramatic Literature in the Seventeenth Century*, Part 2, vol. 2 (Baltimore, 1929–42), say *Rodogune* may have been acted at the end of 1644. Sophie Wilma Deierkauf-Holsboer argues in *Le Théâtre du Marais*, vol. 1 (Paris, 1954), that the cool reception of *La Suite du Menteur* may have caused its withdrawal in favor of *Rodogune* as early as December, 1644.

2. "Que Corneille . . . /Soit encor le Corneille et du *Cid* et d'*Horace*" (*L'Art poétique*, IV.195–96). In the preface to *Pulchérie* Corneille confessed that his characters and their rhetoric were no longer to the taste of the times.

3. See Adam, *Histoire*, vol. 1, pp. 479–80. In France it was a new practice to use the classical Terentian form as a vehicle for quasi-realistic comedy of contemporary manners and, in general, to essay genre mixtures.

"strange monster," made of fragments of several dramatic genres arranged as play-within-play-within-play, for which the closest well-known analogue may be Shakespeare's *The Winter's Tale*.[4]

Médée, Corneille's first tragedy, though reasonably successful and still praised somewhat extravagantly as late as 1800, was at best an awkward reduction of Euripides' barbaric splendors to something like French verisimilitude and decorum. As if conscious that another kind of material would suit him better, Corneille turned to historical legend for the subject of his next composition; and it was with an episode from the wars between feudal Spain and Islam, already dramatized for the Renaissance stage by Guillén de Castro, that he opened the new and greatest era of French dramatic history and the most productive decade of his own life. *Le Cid* became the center of a literary war that raged with increasing bitterness until Richelieu, probably for the sake of his own dignity as patron of the world of letters, as well as for the political reasons generally adduced, imposed an armistice and compelled the young Academy to try the case and pronounce judgment on the play. Corneille perforce submitted, since "the idea of a judicial process seems to divert his excellency," but without by that token recognizing the Academy as a competent authority. In its opinion of Richelieu's tactic, history has generally been on the side of the poet. Still, the case of *Le Cid* remains open and its merits are frequently the subject of modern debate.[5]

In 1640 Corneille broke a silence of three seasons with the tragedy *Horace*, quickly followed by *Cinna* and *Polyeucte*, each an implicit though partial response to charges leveled against *Le Cid*. He had formally adopted classical restrictions, and there is little evidence that they seriously hindered his development.[6] Struggle with his materials as any artist must, he did, and not always with complete

4. On the "Romantic" Corneille revealed in such plays, see Jean Schlumberger, *Plaisir à Corneille* (Paris, 1936), and the corrective: Jacques Morel, "Le jeune Corneille et le théâtre de son temps," *L'Information littéraire* 12 (1950): 185–92. All translations from French or Latin are by the editor of this edition.

5. Lancaster, *History*, Part 2, vol. 1, pp. 128–44, is among the most useful treatments of the episode in English. The bill of charges, drawn up by Jean Chapelain (*Sentiments de l'Académie sur "Le Cid"*) were not wholly groundless, both on the score of formal irregularities—as performances in which the role of the Infanta is omitted tend to show—and on that of character decorum.

6. Corneille's attitude is best summed up by the late E. B. O. Borgerhoff in *The Freedom of French Classicism* (Princeton, 1950), pp. 69 and 70. In *Horace*, at any rate,

success, but the contest itself was a pleasure to be communicated explicitly to the spectator. Not the least of the *merveilles* of his theater was this shared delight in technical difficulties mastered, in great heights scaled. These three plays brought Corneille recognition as the supreme poet of the tragic stage. Rivals and detractors thenceforth modeled their art and their taste on his.

Between *Polyeucte* and *Rodogune* Corneille returned to comedy of character with *Le Menteur* and *La Suite du Menteur*, the former ranked as the best of its kind before *L'Ecole des femmes*; but thereafter he composed no more in the lighter genres. *La Mort de Pompée* in 1643, like *Théodore*, reveals some uncertainty of touch. *Rodogune* however is an excellent example of a new manner, to be maintained until the failure of *Pertharite* (1651) drove the dramatist into a second, longer absence from the theater. The tragedies are based for the most part, like the first Roman plays, on well-known historical sources, but unlike them, they contain characters and actions relatively unknown, even, one might suppose, to the well-read segment of his public, which enables the dramatist to treat them with great freedom. Whereas in *Cinna* and in *Horace* only one among the principal characters is wholly fictional, now, because almost all the action is "invented," [7] the *dramatis personae* are all imaginary, although historical names are retained. It is enough "to begin and to conclude with the historical truth," whereas in between exposition and dénouement the dramatist may invent as he will, even major protagonists. Also significant is the fact that with the increased importance of invention has come a recrudescence of the baroque structure and style of Corneille's pre-*Cid* plays. The plots are extremely intricate or

---

the rules of decorum are obeyed, and the unity of action is observed more strictly than in *Le Cid*, for there are no detachable episodes. But like Rodrigue, Horace faces unrelated perils. See the author's *examen*. On the other hand, *Cinna* and *Polyeucte* are perfectly regular.

7. See the *examens* of *Polyeucte*, *La Mort de Pompée*, and *Héraclius* for Corneille's theory of invention in historical plays. He was doubtless encouraged to treat history with an unexampled freedom in plays from *Rodogune* to *Pertharite* by Guez de Balzac (*Lettre à Corneille*, 17 January 1643): "... I observe that what you lend to history is invariably better than what you have borrowed. The wife of Horace, the betrothed of Cinna ... are indeed your own children ... in whom you are more fortunate than Pompey was in his" [... je prends garde que ce que vous prêtez à l'histoire est toujours meilleur que ce que vous empruntez. La femme d'Horace et la maîtresse de Cinna ... sont deux véritable enfantements.... Vous êtes beaucoup plus heureux en votre race que Pompée en la sienne].

implex, in the author's word: every fiber of the invented intrigue is knitted into a historical background no less complicated than itself and—although Corneille ignores the fact when he can—no less invented, from a certain point of view. He is proud of the ingenuity of these compositions and accepts as a compliment the warning that in performance *Héraclius*, for example, gives one a severe headache.[8] If *Rodogune* shows best what interested the author in 1644 and what drew the public, *Héraclius* (1647) is the extreme example of what subsequently drove it away from this portion of Corneille's work.

Œdipe, commissioned by Foucquet, Louis XIV's Minister of Finance, brought the dramatist back to the theater in 1659 and reverses to some extent the earlier trend toward complexity. Although a subplot involving Dircé (a daughter of Laius) and her lover Thésée doubles the Sophoclean structure, the play remains clear. Like *Le Cid* and *Rodogune*, *Œdipe* is a harbinger, but unlike them, though it was the event of its season, it disappoints posterity. As had happened in *Médée*, the ancient myth is shorn of its mystery, its Attic horror (and anything else that might "distress the delicacy of our ladies") replaced by seventeenth-century political and ethical sentiments not consonant with the dramatic material itself—for example, in Act III, scene v, the astonishing tirade on free will. Corneille returned immediately to history, but with less success than before. Only *Sertorius* strikes approximately the original Cornelian tragic note. Until recently the plays of the last period have been classified as political: the protagonist is a usurper, tyrant, conqueror, or legitimate ruler, and his tirades are studded with *sententiae* appropriate to the princely ethos; his deeds are emblematic of military or political myths useful to King Louis. And like the king, Corneille's new but middle-aged hero is a lover, whenever *raison d'état* permits. In any capacity, he is more pragmatic than passionate; therefore the late plays seemed frigid to the Romantic and unnatural to the Naturalist sensibilities,[9] and they are rarely acted even today. More recently, however, they have drawn critical attention and even a degree of praise seldom accorded since the dramatist's own era.

---

8. In *Héraclius*, as in *Clitandre*, there is a violently tragic situation combined with an almost comically embroiled plot. The heirs to the crown of emperor have been switched in their cradles by their nurse, and the rising action depends on double mistakes of identity.

9. For example, see Adam, *Histoire*, vol. 4, p. 231.

STAGE HISTORY AND SOURCES

Until the end of the eighteenth century *Rodogune* was one of
Corneille's most frequently performed plays, surpassed only by *Le
Cid, Horace, Cinna,* and *Le Menteur.*[10] It was less often seen during the
Romantic era and seldom indeed after 1870, doubtless because the
ruling bourgeoisie of the Third Republic prized Corneille above all
as an illustrator of moral doctrines deemed suitable for *lycée* students;
and *Rodogune,* with its Senecan amoralism, was an embarrassment,
teaching a lesson negatively, if at all. Whereas from 1680 to 1900 an
average of eighteen performances per decade were recorded, during
the second half of the nineteenth century and until 1930 there were
but seven per decade. But from 1930 to the present the average has
risen to ten. The impression of a modest revival since 1945 is strengthened by at least two new productions (independent of repertory performances at the Comédie-Française), one in 1956 and another in 1961.

A reappraisal of the place of *Rodogune* in neoclassical French
theater is clearly overdue. Even though "baroque" is no longer a
term of reproach, something of the Romantics' humanitarian
moralism seems still to inhibit our modern understanding of Corneille's period and therefore stands in the way of an objective study
of his own opinion, expressed in the *examen* of 1660, that he had lent
Rodogune all the individual virtues distributed unequally in his preceding works: it has "a splendid subject, an original and unusual
action, with poetic diction at once striking and natural, a logically
constructed plot, intense pathos, passionate loves and affections, the
whole felicitously composed and carried forward with mounting in-
tensity from act to act," and also, so the passage runs, without in-
fringing the unities. The structural perfection and dramatic force of
the play have never been denied. Nevertheless, for modern criticism
Rodogune's place in the affections of the dramatist has generally
seemed incomprehensible. Certainly no one since Stendhal has
ranked it as Corneille did, superior to the plays of 1640–42. The
latter's admission to the blindness of paternal partiality is therefore

10. See Lancaster, Deierkauf-Holsboer, and Adrien Baillet, in *Jugemens des
sçavans* (Paris, 1685–86), vol. 5, p. 352: ". . . with *Rodogune,* according to general
opinion, Corneille reached his zenith and his solstice, and M. Bayle says (January,
1685) that since then he has held the position." See also E. Champion, *La
Comédie-Française, Année 1937* (Paris, 1937) and A. Joannidès, *La Comédie française
Tableau des représentations par auteurs et par pièces, 1680–1920* (Paris, 1921).

accepted to the letter. By the same token, there is no dispute that, the play being "somewhat more his own" than *Cinna* or *Polyeucte*, to appraise *Rodogune* is to appraise the quintessential manifestation of Cornelian dramaturgy.

The subject is taken, Corneille wrote in the *avertissement* to the first edition in 1647, from the *Roman History* of Appian of Alexandria:[11] Cleopatra, queen of Syria, kills her husband Demetrius II Nicator (Nicanor in the play) from jealousy of Rhodogune, the daughter of Mithridates I and second wife to Demetrius during his long captivity in Parthia. She then assassinates an eldest son, Seleucus, either because he mounted the throne without her permission, or because he intended to avenge his father's death, or because she was moved by an insane rage against everyone. Later, Antiochus, the second son, becomes king and forces his mother to drink a cup of poison she had prepared for him. "That is what history lent me." From Appian the dramatist has retained little but names and places, certain episodes antecedent to the action, and what Corneille has called its effects: the killing of Seleucus, the death by poison of Cleopatra, and the succession to the crown of the surviving Antiochus. But these events are made to arise from different causes and are brought about in a different manner. Mentioned also as minor or negligible historical sources are the first book of Maccabees, the *Jewish Antiquities* of Flavius Josephus, and the *Universal History* of Justin. Josephus supplied expository detail for Laonice's narrative of Nicanor's captivity in Parthia, the revolt of Tryphon, and Cleopatra's marriage to her brother-in-law, Antiochus Sidetes. Justin, avers Corneille, recounts her tragic story in greater detail but quite differently: Nicanor was murdered by a certain Alexander Zabinas, not by his wife. Therefore, regarding characterizations and conflicts between the exposition and the conclusion of *Rodogune*, historical documents provide no model. The disguises or alterations of history, as Corneille terms them, are "fictions . . . invented embellishments . . . probable causes of the unnatural effects found in history which I am not permitted by the laws of poetry to alter." [12]

This account of the sources and the dramatist's manner of utilizing them in the composition of *Rodogune* remains an article of faith with most modern editors of the play (see note 16, below) although it has

11. See Appendix for notes on the historical sources.
12. Aristotle *Poetics* xiv.10. See Corneille, *Discours du poème dramatique*, as well as the *examens* already noted, for his own interpretation of the classical rule.

long been known that history lent somewhat more than he said. Of course Corneille has created for his Cleopatra a situation in which the original of the portrait did not find herself, nor were Appian's Seleucus and Antiochus the affectionate brotherly rivals for crown and the hand of Rodogune that they became in the play. But it is not true that the historical record of the era supplied no germinal source for the fictions. A clue to the actual genesis lies in a more than fortuitous resemblance between the account given of this play and that of *Le Cid*. In the *avertissements* to both, Corneille quotes and discusses at what would seem to be unnecessary length historical sources that indeed have very little to do with the plays, while granting but a brief mention to others that have as it were almost everything. His reasons are obvious. The Renaissance practice of imitation, or adaptation of literary models, was falling into disrepute, and Corneille meant, in the case of *Le Cid*, simply to cover himself against the charge of plagiarism. To the naïve, his play might have seemed but an easy copy of *Las mocedades del Cid*. Similarly, he concealed the major source of *Rodogune*, perhaps in part because he doubted his contemporaries' ability to see that a mosaic of fragments drawn from Justin, Josephus, and Appian, shuffled and redistributed to suit a purely dramatic purpose, is better proof of originality than would have been the entirely imaginery design he claims to have embroidered on the historical fabric of Appian alone. Furthermore, Corneille nervously anticipated a cold reception by the erudite, who might have scolded him even more severely for a quite free arrangement of "fact" than they could have for a purely fictional interpolation.

L. Riddle[13] was among the first to note that Corneille had not acknowledged his indebtedness to Justin for several prominent features, for example the portrayal of Cleopatra as a woman driven entirely by ambition, and not by the jealousy of Rodogune that Appian attributed to her, and especially the idea of Rodogune coming to Syria where she would be imprisoned by a rival. Unfortunately, Riddle missed the true sources of the latter idea, as he did, in fact, numerous other links, and the line of investigation he opened has not been followed since. No doubt to retrace the first steps in the composition of *Rodogune* it is necessary to read Justin as the dramatist himself was able to do, guided by historiographical traditions in which the search for structural and figural analogies still played a

---

13. In *The Genesis and Sources of P. Corneille's Tragedies from "Médée" to "Pertharite"* (Baltimore, 1926).

part. In three particularly important instances he was exegete, taking not only what is in, but also what can be inferred from his text.

Extensive analysis would be inappropriate here, but since *Rodogune* is a moot play to some degree because the extent and nature of Justin's contribution is not known, a brief chronology, with excerpts from the *Universal History* and additional comment, is given as an appendix to this edition. For present purposes, two examples of Corneille's method will suffice.

First, it must be noted that the idea of Rodogune coming to Syria as Nicanor's queen was not the brain-child of the dramatist. It was first conceived by Mithridates I, her father, who "with royal magnanimity gave [the captured Nicanor] royal honors and his daughter to wife, and promised to restore to him the Syrian kingdom, held by Tryphon in his absence."[14] The same plan was formed also, after Mithridates' death, by his son Phraates, on no less than two separate occasions. Thus the exact circumstances put together by the dramatist might have arisen in history, but for the minor accident of a revolt of Phraates' Scythian mercenaries.[15] Since Cleopatra herself had come to Syria in that very fashion, imposed on Nicanor by a father intent upon controlling Syrian affairs through his children, she, and Corneille after her, could not have failed to understand that should Nicanor return on the crest of a Parthian invasion, she would lose her crown, if not her life, and that Rodogune would then rule in her stead. The play is a dramatization of the historical Cleopatra's recurrent nightmare.

The most remarkable illustration of Corneille's method of deriva-

14. Justin, XXXVIII. In 1647 Corneille claimed the paternity of his title-heroine with the phrase "... [I have made] Rodogune [Cleopatra's] prisoner, although she never came to Syria." In the *examen* of 1660 he has changed his stance: "... history does not say what became of Rodogune after the death of Demetrius, who was probably bringing her with him to Syria." In the historical circumstances that would not in fact have been possible. Evidently he argues the contrary because other readers had pointed out what he intended still to conceal: to carry out his purpose, Mithridates would have had to depose the daughter of the Ptolemies and make a daughter of the Arsacides queen of Syria. Therefore, the central fiction of the play was not quite a creation *ex nihilo*. In this connection, it is worthy of note that in the *examen* of 1660 Justin is no longer depreciated as a less reliable authority than Appian.

15. Corneille makes of this negligible incident a war with Armenia, and he has it occur later, to provide a reason for Phraates' improbable, not to say impossibly stupid, decision to leave his sister helpless in the hands of a murderous rival.

tion by inference is found in the source of his much and deservedly admired fifth act. Again, in one of those repeated cycles of which later Seleucid history seems primarily composed, after the deaths of Nicanor and Seleucus, a foreign wife was imposed on the king of Syria (Antiochus, surnamed Grypus, ruling conjointly with his mother) by a foreign king intent upon having a hand in the country. This was another Cleopatra, surnamed Tryphaena, a niece of Cleopatra Thea, and from whose story in Justin Corneille has drawn many features of the play. Here it is the probable consequences of her union with Antiochus, not formulated explicitly by any of Corneille's sources, that must be kept in mind:

> Seleucus . . . was slain by his mother because he had assumed the diadem without her leave. The other [Antiochus], surnamed Grypus . . . was made king by the mother, but in such manner that while the title belonged to the son, supreme authority remained in the hands of the mother . . . . Ptolemy . . . sent to Grypus both support and his daughter [Cleopatra] Tryphaena in marriage. Grypus, having recovered his ancestors' kingdom and surmounted the external dangers, was then attacked by his treacherous mother . . . who, greedy for power . . . and seeing with pain that his triumph diminished her authority, offered him a poisoned cup when he came in from exercise. But Grypus, forewarned of her treachery, as if to vie with her in courtesy, commands that she drink it herself. She refusing, he insists. Then producing a witness, he argues that she has no defense but to prove her innocence by drinking herself what she had offered her son. Thus the queen is vanquished: the crime falls back on herself as she dies by the poison prepared for another (Justin, XXXIX).

The parallel of Justin's account and the last act of *Rodogune* is obvious. Moreover, the arrangement of details and—to use a phrase frequent in Corneille's writings—the probable causes of the incident suggest that this passage is possibly the single most important source for the entire play. It is unlikely that Justin's Antiochus would have offended his redoubtable mother unless urged and supported by someone as ruthlessly ambitious and as ferocious as she. That is, Cleopatra would not have seen her influence wane and would not have attempted to assassinate her son had she not discovered a rival in her daughter-in-law Tryphaena. Finally, it is but a small exercise

of the imagination to infer that Tryphaena was present at the death
of Cleopatra, playing a part not unlike that of Rodogune in the
play.[16]

Mithridates' intention to restore Nicanor to the throne of Syria
with Rodogune at his side and the probable conflict of Cleopatra
with her daughter-in-law gave the dramatist not only an occasional
detail, but taken together, the scheme of the first and fifth acts of his
new tragedy. The rising action, the rivalry of brothers forced to
stand between their mother and their beloved, and that of princesses
homicidally bent on revenge, remains to be accounted for. The motifs
are commonplace individually in drama and history alike. Compositions like *Rodogune* combining them all are rare. In Justin's account of
Antiochus' reign after Cleopatra's death there appears however just
such a four-sided conflict and just such a civil war as was foreseen by
Seleucus in lines 175–76 (I.iii). The actors are Antiochus Grypus,
his half-brother Antiochus Cyzicenus, and their wives, Cleopatra
Tryphaena and her sister, Cleopatra IV. The hatred and cruelty of
Tryphaena toward her sister, her demands that Grypus be the instru-
ment of her vengeance (a motif that appears doubled in the play, as
in fact do all motifs) the terms of his refusal, her jealous rage and
the subsequent murder of Cleopatra IV on Tryphaena's own orders—
all this cannot be foreign to the gestation of *Rodogune*.[17]

In conclusion, there is evidence to justify the hypothesis that,
echoes of other plays such as *Médée* and *Le Cid*[18] aside, *Rodogune* is a

16. French writers on ancient history (see Appendix) and a recent editor of the
play (see Corneille, *Rodogune*, ed. M. Cégretin [Rennes: Bordas, 1964]) have noted
in passing the resemblance of Justin's account of Cleopatra's death to Corneille's
dénouement. It may be argued however that no one, not even the dramatist, would
have inferred a possibility of Tryphaena's share in it without an antecedent knowledge of the play. It might seem unlikely, therefore, that Justin's text inspired
Corneille to fuse the historical Tryphaena and Rodogune. On the other hand,
Corneille's preference for working from sources in the manner suggested here,
stimulated often by the slightest of hints, has been well documented.

17. The larger aspects of structure aside, there is a profusion of echoes of every
kind (episodes, character traits, rhetoric) inexplicable by coincidence alone.

18. Lancaster's interesting suggestion (*History*, Part II, vol. 2, p. 498) that in *La
Mort de Pompée* and *Théodore* there can be seen an attempt to repeat the successes of
Cinna and *Polyeucte* might well be extended. With *Rodogune* the dramatist reopened
the vein not of *Médée*, as Riddle argued, but of his first great triumph. Differences of
setting and ethos distort to the view many underlying similarities of element and
principles of composition, as well as the apparent effort to employ the same

contaminatio of three historical narratives. Appian's version of Cleopatra's life is the least of them, although it may have been the first to attract the dramatist's attention, for it reads like a play synopsis; doubtless it furnished the jealousy and thirst for vengeance he attributes to Cleopatra as a hypocritical pretense. But clearly the structural idea for the most characteristic feature of *Rodogune*, the dance-like semi-incestuous pattern of double rivalries, came from Justin, especially from the scene of Cleopatra's death—the outcome, it can be inferred, of her struggle with her daughter-in-law—and from the story of her two surviving sons and their wives, in which one son plays a part much like that of Corneille's Antiochus, who attempts to appease and to reconcile the furious women.[19]

It is unfortunate that Corneille felt obliged to claim his play as a product of the poetic imagination in a sense that it was not, rather than as the achievement of Renaissance imitation which it is.[20] It is impressively the more brilliant the more comprehensively one divines the complexities of its relation to the sources. This and not *Héraclius* is the most *spirituel* of his plays.[21]

THE PLAY

If it is true, as it is sometimes said, that the plot in seventeenth-century French tragedy is negligible, it is partly because during the late Renaissance emphasis shifted from the pathos of a great fall or from the catastrophe itself to the psychological or moral causes of catastrophe. Plots may therefore be composed entirely of verbal incident and may be concluded on internal or subjective peripeties, or, in rare cases, on none at all. When every passion has been discovered, and when the ethic of each character is finally manifest, the

---

thaumaturgical powers of which Corneille's arch rival, Georges Scudéri, complained in his *Observations sur "Le Cid"* (Paris, 1637). There is in the earlier play also a four-sided conflict (composed of two triangles), but the Don Sanche part is a mere sketch. *Rodogune*, in this perspective, is as it were a more complete set of variations on a similar theme.

19. Even the innocence of Antiochus is at least inferrable from Justin's version of Cleopatra's death. There is no explicit statement that force was employed, nor is it certain that his Antiochus foresaw, when he ordered his mother to demonstrate her innocence, that she would prefer death to defeat.

20. In his prefaces and *examens* Corneille attaches to the term "invention" something of the modern connotation.

21. See the *examen* of *Héraclius*. *Spirituel* here means ingenious.

play is over. The spending of passion and the resolution of conflict have left the protagonists roughly where they were at the beginning, minus the original motive of action. *Cinna* is such a play. *Rodogune* is not, of course, a pure example. Indeed, it is constructed so as best to prepare for a striking dénouement, where conflicts are resolved for the title-heroine, but not without loss of life, or worse, for others. On the other hand, all the few changes of fortune, all the decisive, irremediable actions, are delayed until the last act, which means that in the first four the plot is composed of verbal revelations entirely. Each reveals a motive and a choice; therefore every incident of the plot is at one and the same time a detail of characterization, and the two elements can be studied together.

As regards external form, *Rodogune* is quite regular, and little comment is required, except on the exposition, the only part of the plot proper that has been adversely criticized.

Laonice's historical resumé in Act I has been called useless, improbable, and aesthetically displeasing. Even if her brother Timagenes, tutor to Cleopatra's two sons, had been unable to piece together the story of recent Syrian events for himself before leaving Egypt, where he had accompanied his charges and educated them in the safety of their uncle's court, he would have attempted to satisfy his curiosity before the wedding and coronation day upon which the play opens. Even for spectators, Laonice's first narratives are of little utility, for her information, the events that led to the assassination of Cleopatra's husband Demetrius Nicator (or Nicanor, as Corneille rebaptizes him), will be recounted in detail on no less than three more occasions. Finally, since the first narrative has no practical effect on Timagenes or on his subsequent behavior, both it and he are termed "cold."[22]

Objections of this kind are not easily answered in the critical vocabulary of the era, and Corneille himself seemed to agree that the first and fourth scene narratives of Act I of *Rodogune* were mere vestiges of early Renaissance rhetorical tragedy and that it would have been better to eliminate them. But, he lamented, "natural seeming" expositions are almost impossible in historical plays.

He had managed, however, better than he was willing to claim. Taking the complaints in reverse order, plays that are constructed to

---

22. L'abbé François d'Aubignac, *La Pratique du théâtre* (Paris, 1657), is representative of the critical disapproval. Corneille responds in the *examens* of *Rodogune* and *Héraclius*.

become increasingly more violent from start to finish must open on scenes of relative calm; it is merely pedantic to argue that every character must have an immediate, emotional response to every word spoken in his presence. Timagenes is cold in the first act, but he has no reason to be otherwise. He need be only an interested, attentive listener, for Laonice's story brings quite enough excitement to the stage. Nor is there much point in raising the issue of verisimilitude. When Timagenes asks for the story is of no consequence, provided the natural order of events is not violated, for days and years in the Cornelian cosmos are abstract, having neither quantity nor powers; in passing they neither heal wounds nor leave wrinkles.[23] Finally, the major objection, that Laonice's narration is useless, seems substantial, but it too collapses under scrutiny. Every version of an incident narrated as many times as the death of Nicanor must have a function of its own. In this case all versions, including the first, which the audience, like Timagenes, is inclined to trust implicitly in accord with a well-established dramatic convention, are designed to have ambivalence, or better, polyvalence: they are given one value for the narrator, another for his interlocutor, sometimes a third for a stage "audience" (as in Act V) and, more rarely, still a fourth for the audience proper. For everyone, every revision of the past is meant to transform the present, as from point to point various motives are ascribed for the murder and different passions are alleged to have arisen from it.[24] Corneille alluded many times to the superiority of expositions that are dramatic in themselves. It is dangerous to assume that he has yet to master the rudiments of his craft. The point of expository narratives that no one needs merely for the information emerges when Laonice, ostensibly Cleopatra's confidante, proves to be the first victim of the queen's impostures. The explanation of Nicanor's death given by Laonice is erroneous and it therefore becomes a danger to Rodogune. Moreover Laonice is misled regarding Cleopatra's future intentions, an error that might well have had consequences fatal to herself. The discovery in Act II, that the queen wishes Rodogune dead, brings to the confidante a belated awareness of her own danger. She quickly abandons the target of the queen's wrath, alleging the duty of fidelity to her

---

23. Exceptions in Corneille's theater are required by a source.
24. For a partly different explication see Robert J. Nelson, *Corneille, His Heroes and Their Worlds* (Philadelphia, 1963), p. 139.

mistress. For these and other reasons the tutor and the lady-in-waiting are figures of dramatic irony. Timagenes turned to his sister for a "true history" just as the unfolding of Cleopatra's stratagems is about to demonstrate her unreliability and ignorance. He too has a share in the drama. Neither is a mere analogue of the protatic messenger of early Renaissance tragedy, of the passive [25] alter ego of the protagonist. Moreover in their dialogue, which seems at first little more than the gossip of courtiers, they establish a basic structural unit and a major thematic figure of *Rodogune*: the discovery of secrets and dramatic irony. Every character, except for the supernumerary Orontes, is developed in this unit and this figure. Although Cleopatra does not appear in the first act, her role can be considered immediately from this point of view.

First, the action rises or is complicated almost entirely by actions of the queen, in default of sustained enterprise on the part of her antagonists, whose reactions are invariably resolved into inaction. Cleopatra's secret purpose is to retain possession of the scepter, and she is a danger to Rodogune only in as much as Rodogune is an obstacle to that purpose: a treaty with Parthia requires that Cleopatra abdicate in favor of her eldest son and marry him to Rodogune, thus bringing to an end her influence in Syria. But misled by Laonice and consequently without the knowledge to interpret precisely the queen's first tirade, we do not see the meaning of her words. Moreover, the overt conflict has seemed to materialize in the apparent or secondary motifs of jealousy and revenge, which in fact provide Cleopatra with her tactics, calculated to draw to mutual destruction all who contest her supremacy, whether intentionally or unintentionally. Seleucus warns in the pathetic tirade of Act I, scene iii, that Cleopatra will only need to fan the very flames that destroyed Troy and Thebes, that is, to exacerbate the rivalry of himself and his twin brother for the crown that hangs between them, subject to maternal caprice, and for the hand of Rodogune, loved equally by both. But the very same scene reveals how Cleopatra will be frustrated: Antiochus and Seleucus are bound by an incorruptible fraternal love, and they agree to be rivals only in magnanimity and generosity. Each will be satisfied, whatever may befall, to find his

---

25. Jacques Scherer in *La dramaturgie classique en France* (Paris, 1950), p. 49, mentions Laonice's third-act warning to Rodogune as an early exception to the rule that confidant(e)s take no active part in the action.

own good fortune in that of his brother. If the first act has a fault, it is the necessary but anticlimactic passivity of the princes. Their heroic good faith reduces them to inaction, and blunts the point of Seleucus' allusion to the Trojan and Theban wars almost before it is made. Without Cleopatra the act is static, and the best parts of it are those usually criticized: Laonice's historical narratives are as brilliant as any in Corneille; and there are appropriately lyrical counterparts in the scene of Rodogune's doubtful hope in the bright future evoked by Laonice and in the delicate allusions to a new fear, the nightmare of princesses, that political necessity will put them in the wrong bed—for she secretly prefers Antiochus to his brother.[26]

From the queen's first appearance in Act II the drama has an accelerated rhythm and a constantly rising "temperature," for Cleopatra has no peer among those wilful tragic protagonists who without the least inner resistance explore evil to the limit of credible human nature—without, on the other hand, sinking into satanism, bestiality, or madness—except perhaps for Lady Macbeth in the early scenes of Shakespeare's play. Cleopatra, however, does not throughout the play swerve from her course; she never falters, she is never passive, and thus there is little shading or depth to provide relief. For a moment in Act III it seems that Rodogune may take the initiative from her, when she too urges Antiochus and Seleucus to avenge their father's death, offering her hand to the more dutiful son, but the impression is quickly dispelled. Although Act III is wholly a mirror-image of Act II, it is ultimately without consequence of its own, except for strengthening Seleucus' determination to resign his claims to the throne and to Rodogune. In effect, only Cleopatra gives motion to the play or acts to some credible purpose; and Rodogune, who shares the fourth act with her, has in the end no course but to rescind her demands for vengeance, substituting an avowal of love for Antiochus and the wish that he not return to her presence until he has acquired the crown by some means more laudable than parricide. The scene of this revelation is modeled closely on *Le Cid*, Act V, scene i, with the difference that Chimène's words alter Rodrigue's intentions, whereas Rodogune's speech has no effect on Antiochus but to raise his spirits, for he continues to pursue his set goal by means already decided: to soften the queen's

26. See note to line 367 (I.v).

wrath by appealing to her better nature. The scene in question therefore gives no motion to the plot, for Cleopatra is an emblem of evil:
she has no better nature within the reach of human appeal. She lacks
all feeling, whether for husband, children, religion, or morality, and
nothing is left in her but the rage of frustrated ambition and hatred
of all who stand between her and the crown. Two lines on *Nature*,
tendresse (lines 1491 and 1511) as she plans the assassination of her
children tend rather to accentuate the harshness of the portrait. She
is a monolith, an immense, single force driving irresistibly to the
predestined fall. Doubtless Cleopatra fascinates, like a basilisk, but
she repels also. It is difficult to discover in oneself curiosity or even
pity for what lies beneath her scaly armor. Precisely for these reasons the seventeenth century found her as *admirable* as the good
Antiochus; and later certain Romantics, like Stendhal, with their
characteristic penchant for aesthetic contemplation of *le beau crime*,
appreciated *Rodogune* on this account. Cleopatra however might have
been intolerable even to them were it not for the art of the characterization.

The principal device is ironic self-revelation, in which Cleopatra's
character and motives are manifest on three levels. In soliloquy, as
she apostrophizes herself or her diadem, the irony is reflective or
lyrical, communicating self-knowledge, an unconceptualized awareness that her crimes, both remembered and foreseen, surpass the
alleged causes. That is, for her, ambition is an absolute, not the con-
tingency but the ground of her existence. She is ambition itself. The
irony is in her awareness that she is playing, for herself as well as for
others, the role of deserted and jealous wife. From the soliloquies her
actual emotions and intentions can be correctly divined, and they
provide a fixed frame of reference in which all other roles can be
coordinated. Dialogue in the court scenes of the second and fifth
acts is ironic in the second degree, properly dramatic, for the queen's
rhetoric, following a related soliloquy, is clear to the audience but
equivocally ambiguous for her interlocutors. The form and sense of
her phrases are at odds: an irony engaged in dialectic with itself.
Antiochus and Seleucus suspect they understand, but they dare not
understand what they suspect, as Cleopatra turns their world inside
out. On the surface she is benevolent, then sadistic as she forces them
to responses that war with common knowledge, common sense, and
with their natures. Whatever lingering pity a spectator may feel for
her is dissolved by this extraordinarily cruel scene. Finally, Cleopatra

is furious and openly menacing. Yet even when they see that Syria's throne is to be bought with Rodogune's death, Cleopatra has concealed part of her purpose. The third degree of irony, quasi-epic, is reached in the private conversations of the queen and one or the other of her sons: every intention and emotion is manifest to the audience but entirely concealed from her partner in the dialogue. The spectator cannot—it is the design of the dramatist that he should not—immediately and distinctly perceive the separate levels of self-revelation, for that would be to lessen the baroque contrast of Cleopatra's fixed goal and sinuously shifting angle of attack. As it is, Corneille has achieved in *Rodogune* through rhetoric alone a striking but subtle tour de force of sustained dramatic tension, subsumed in the final irony of the play itself. As in Cleopatra's own case, so for her antagonists, whose every effort to avert disaster brings it closer. She is a victim of her own acts, as Seleucus is of his withdrawal from the contest, and as Antiochus will be of his inaction, which may be said to have caused the deaths of the former indirectly.

Until the last act the queen, like the others, seems paradoxically to stand still, a brooding presence, the violence of her speech notwithstanding. Her threats are indirect and, given the immediate resistance of her sons, not precise in aim. Would the dramatist in fact have entitled the tragedy after her, had he not been uncertain, as he avers in the dedication, of the effect on the public of two Cleopatras in succession? A general absence of direction in the behavior of all characters of the drama suggests, as does especially the early collapse of fraternal rivalry, that *Rodogune* does not illustrate theme, subject, or character quite as *Othello* does jealousy, *Cinna* imperial clemency, *Phèdre* Phèdre. Commonplaces of love, ambition, jealousy, revenge, *raison d'état* and so forth are on every lip, but there they hang, neutralizing each other, from which is to be inferred not of course that the play is a concoction of rhetoric, but rather a coordinated scansion system. That is, the drama places humanity in an extreme situation and observes successively the diversity of reaction. If subject there be, strictly speaking, it is masks, or better, the fear of masks; which means that in *Rodogune* Corneille has come more nearly than he had before and more interestingly than he would again to one of the central themes of tragedy and comedy, that of mistaken identity. Thus the question, Whose tragedy is it? is not merely academic.

"All the tragic action falls on Cleopatra," according to the dedication, but perhaps the tragedy does not bear her name because in a double-centered action she is too much executioner, or not enough victim. The actual structure, with its intersecting triangles of love, revenge, and ambition, allows several possibilities. The princess herself, though she survives, supports in her way the tragic action, and moreover she illustrates the Aristotelian rule that heroes be good, but not too good. Therefore, though the actual catastrophe may not arise either from her flaw or from her acts, her claims to the title cannot be set aside.

On the other hand, Antiochus is a promising candidate for several reasons. Like Cinna, in the tragedy so named, although Antiochus is not the direct source of conflict he is the stake in the game: Syria will be ruled by Cleopatra or Rodogune through him, and the actual shape of the crisis is determined by stances that he adopts. He alone pursues a fixed goal, in opposition to Cleopatra: the reconciliation of glory and love,[27] and the avoidance of tragedy. He fails to reach it not from weakness of will but from pride. An easy victory over Rodogune's spirit of vengeance induces in him that overweening optimism perennially the source of tragic falls. It traps him into relying exclusively on the rhetoric of emotional appeal in the coming contest with Cleopatra. Had he attended to Seleucus, who counseled open rebellion (lines 744–47), there might have been no tragedy.[28] But also, in the algebra of seventeenth-century dramaturgy, Seleucus must expiate the impiety of revolt against a royal parent, and thus his death leaves Antiochus to make an innocent conquest of throne and princess. At the same time, the final catastrophe forces Antiochus to recognize human blindness and, perhaps, the emptiness of triumphs that cost him a brother and a mother. Antiochus is the witness of a destroyed world. He alone illustrates the complete Fergussonian triad, purpose-passion-perception, requisite in protagonists who are able to enlist and retain one's sympathy.[29]

The dramatist presumably discarded the possibility of centering the play more firmly on Antiochus because the latter, though busy,

---

27. See note 19 above, and note to *Acteurs*, line 1, below.

28. Judd D. Hubert, "The Conflict between Chance and Morality in *Rodogune*," *Modern Language Notes* 74 (1959): 234–39, and Nelson, *Corneille*, p. 148, emphasize the discordant quality of Seleucus. The latter finds him the only tragic figure of the play. See also Leonard Wang, "The 'Tragic' Theatre of Corneille," *The French Review* 25 (January, 1952): 182–91.

29. The parts of the tragic *agon* have thus been named by Francis Fergusson in *The Idea of a Theater* (Princeton, 1949), pp. 13–26.

is somewhat undersized. Both history and dramatic conception require that he be ineffectual, at times inexplicable, to such an extent that he has been dismissed by at least one commentator as a sniveling fool. At best Antiochus seems disquietingly diplomatic, too willing to gloss over the bloody past and the vengeful present and to profit by the one if he can elude the other. Not before the last act does he exhibit the natural simplicity of Seleucus.[30] Antiochus therefore can be appraised only as part of a complete picture, and for that reason alone he makes a poor title-hero by himself.

It is appropriate to ask whether there may not be a reason to consider the names of both the brothers as a possible title. However, entitling the play *Antiochus and Seleucus* or *Les frères rivaux* or *ennemis* would be misleading. Although the situation is oedipal in appearance, the brothers exhibit none of the emotions or inhibitions associated with the term, either with respect to their parents or each other. Corneille has almost certainly drawn their portraits from an ordinary pair of brothers, not from actual twins, and so realistically that some spectators may unconsciously determine which has the prior right of birth even before Cleopatra's disclosure in Act IV.[31] At that point, incidentally, her word has no value, and in effect the revelation is never made. Seleucus, in whom it is tempting to see Pierre Corneille himself, is characteristically an elder son: self-reliant, rebellious, and quick to react against unreasonable demands. His advice to seize the throne and decide the questions of succession and marriage for themselves is that of a brother accustomed to dominance; and he is open, even brusque, in expressing doubts or revulsion. On the other hand, he is inclined to silence when his opinions are rejected. A moral being, as distinct from morally perceptive, Seleucus steps away from intolerable choices and is killed as he retreats. Antiochus is a typical second son, flexible but persistent, and given to concealed reactions; unwilling to stand openly opposed, he risks the arts of emotional persuasion, even on those from whom he ought to expect the worst.

---

30. Note, however, that Antiochus' final experience of moral revulsion is foreshadowed in lines 1070–80 (III.v).

31. Some contemporary psychologists, systematizing common observations, believe that a child's place in the sequence of brothers and sisters more profoundly influences the development of his personality than oedipal relationships. Quite possibly Seleucus and Antiochus are in a very general way portraits of Corneille himself and his brother Thomas. They certainly do not exhibit the traits expected in identical twins.

Also, he is more apt to attract proud, strong-minded women like Rodogune, not to speak of Cleopatra, with whom he was willing, like his historical counterpart, to rule jointly. To the first, he is a more subtle challenge than Seleucus, and to the second a greater danger. The princess's lyrical allusion to "sympathy" is not a vapor from the sentimental, feminine soul; it is a practical recognition that Antiochus' character balances and harmonizes with her own.

Rodogune is in the last analysis the correct choice for the title. Although her two suitors are the stake in her contest with the queen, they have necessarily unequal weights and functions in the play. It is clear almost from the beginning that one of the two roles is to be preponderant, and, moreover, that Antiochus and Seleucus are not to be developed as active rivals. Indeed, after the third act they do not appear together. Rodogune has paradoxically accomplished the queen's purpose. She has driven them apart.

Of Cleopatra Thea, Bevan rightly observed, ". . . in the person of the young princess Destiny was introducing the Erinys of the house of Seleucus."[32] To designate the central function of the Parthian protagonist Bevan's metaphor may be extended. In the person of Rodogune, Corneille was introducing Cleopatra's Nemesis: "What spells have you wrought, detestable woman!" she cries (line 1480), when it is clear that Rodogune has taken her children, as she had taken their father, and as she would indirectly take her life. But no one understands this invention of Corneille, or at least no one has been able to explain her to the entire satisfaction of those who do not, and the tragedy stands or falls, in the estimation of the critical public, with her. Many echoes and a certain structural resemblance tempt one to think that with his Parthian princess Corneille had in mind to try his hand once more at the magic of *Le Cid*. Whether that is so, it is a fact that because of her character flames rose immediately from the ashes of the old quarrel, and have died out only to burst forth anew as recently as 1949.[33] Indeed the later play is a better topic for debate. It gives no cause for more or less sterile argument about the

32. Edwyn R. Bevan, *The House of Seleucus* (New York: Barnes and Noble, Inc., 1966), vol. 2, p. 212. This is a revision of the first edition published in 1902 (London).

33. See René Jasinski, "Psychologie de Rodogune," *Revue d'histoire littéraire de la France* 49 (1949), nos. 3 and 4, pp. 209–19 and 322–38, and Louis Herland, "A propos de Rodogune," *ibid.* (1951), no. 1, p. 126.

unities, nor are there anecdotal curiosities to distract one from the issues of some theoretical significance.

The dramatist defines Rodogune as a virtuous person, and so she seems to be in the first act. So also she proves to have been as the play ends. But in the central section her efforts to incite Antiochus and Seleucus to matricide tempts one to agree with the latter: "A soul so cruel deserved a mother like ours—from that womb she ought to have come!" (lines 1051–52). The princess attempts to justify herself in later scenes, and in effect she withdraws her heinous demands. The impression remains, however, of a harsh, unsympathetic, and basically immoral character, and one is prepared to credit as natural, though not to share fully, the immediate belief of Antiochus, after Seleucus' dying accusation of "a hand once loved," in the possibility of Rodogune's guilt. Corneille patently hoped that a dénouement proving her innocence would in retrospect lend credibility to the withdrawal in Act IV of her demand for Cleopatra's blood. But his expectation is not, and in the nature of the case cannot be, fulfilled. For many spectators one or the other, the virtuous shows of the first and fifth acts or the criminal incitements of the third, will remain unassimilable in this otherwise remorselessly logical and coherent work.

Three main lines of argument have been explored in critical literature on the character of Rodogune,[34] the easiest of access being that all difficulties can be eliminated in performance. Without forcing the text, an actress can bring out villainy, hypocrisy, or both. Or the exotic Parthian aspect of the role can be intensified, so that

34. Quoted or paraphrased are: Saint-Evremond, *Défense de "Rodogune" à M. de Barillon* (1677), and Nelson, *Corneille*, pp. 154–55, who see Rodogune as oriental or Machiavellian and therefore not really immoral; Adam, *Histoire*, vol. 2, pp. 360–61, and André Stegmann, *L'Héroïsme cornélien, genèse et signification*, vol. 2 (Paris, 1968), p. 599, who judge Rodogune a fit match for Cleopatra in her criminal intention; Lancaster, *History*, Part 2, vol. 2, and F. Tanquerey, *Le Romanesque dans le théâtre de Corneille* (Paris, 1939), pp. 23–25, who hold Rodogune to be immoral, but allege extenuating circumstances: she is ". . . prematurely soured, furious, and impotent." Herland's suggestion (below) that she is an innocent vehicle of Nicanor's ghost is found in "L'Imprévisible et l'Inexplicable dans la conduite du Héros comme Ressort Tragique chez Corneille" in *Le Théâtre tragique*, ed. Jean Jacquot (Paris, 1962). Octave Nadal, in *Le Sentiment de l'amour dans l'œuvre de Pierre Corneille* (Paris, 1948), pp. 224–25, starting from the critique of Voltaire (see following note), hypothesizes a genuine romance of Nicanor and Rodogune, a transfer of love from father to son, etc. But Nadal's belief, that the discordant elements of Corneille's plot were forced on him by history, is of course untenable.

obscurity, from the seventeenth-century occidental point of view, becomes an essential aspect of the characterization, in which case spectators need not attempt to measure Rodogune by their own ethical standards.

According to the second interpretation, sometimes combined with the first, Rodogune's third-act behavior is Machiavellian, that is to say, in the context reasonable, even praiseworthy. The morality of kings is not that of the rest of mankind. They may be called upon to defend themselves by means that in the ordinary citizen would be criminal. By 1644 royal prerogative and the dilemmas of *raison d'état* had long been a staple of tragedy, and furthermore, during the coming Fronde the subject would be exhaustively debated by political pamphleteers. It can be argued, therefore, that the so-called incoherence of *Rodogune* is in fact a faithful reflection of the immiscibility of public and private ethics and does not disturb sophisticated spectators of the era. Corneille provided an interesting variation of this defense, one that rests on a similar literary and dramatic convention: a royal princess cannot admit fear simply or sincerely, in order to gain protection from a suitor. The latter must always adopt the attitude of a supplicant, and she must always be enabled to accept his service as her due. Corneille means to say, I think, that Rodogune's proposal to Antiochus and Seleucus, vengeance for their father and her own erstwhile betrothed, must be understood as the sort of conundrum-like demand for which the contemporary literature of preciosity had prepared the playgoer, who can be counted upon to understand that an *amant généreux* is enjoined less often to literal mindless obedience than to the invention of strategies whereby moral custom and law, love and pride can be satisfied at one stroke. When Seleucus condemns Rodogune out of hand, he disqualifies himself as a suitor: he is faithless, he is wanting in courage, persistence, and ingenuity. The principal force of this interpretation is lent by the fact that it lays a convincing base for the rhetoric of Rodogune's actual recantation in Act IV.

The third defense opens, appropriately, with a Parthian retreat. Admitting that the characterization is irremediably obscure, its advocates point to the claim that Cleopatra having dishonored the treaty with Parthia, Rodogune herself must fulfill an obligation of revenge for Nicanor that she had abjured in the name of that treaty. If all she says in the third act soliloquy comes from a genuine sense of duty and not from the need to justify her conduct, her demands on the princes are virtuous and she consistent throughout.

All such arguments fail to convince for various reasons that may take various forms, but are reducible to the one basic fact: the characterization of Rodogune is clarifiable only at the expense of another role or of the structure of the play itself. If she is but another Senecan "horror queen," or if she is merely an incomprehensible Parthian, the central rivalry is psychologically uninteresting, and Antiochus is made to seem either despicable or obscure. The modes of creating the role for the stage suggested above would bring the play perilously close to black comedy, which was not an option of the seventeenth-century tragic stage in France. And in arguments from *Il Principe*, there is little but after-the-fact rationalization. Political maxims do not alter unpalatable domestic realities: a woman has urged her suitors, one of whom she claims to love, to matricide. Moreover, as Voltaire noted regarding the similar action of the queen, this Machiavellianism is absurd, as the reactions of both brothers prove. Finally, the third suggestion, that a religious duty to the spirit of the dead king absolves Rodogune from the sin of personal complicity, is ill supported by the text. Several echoes of *Le Cid* in Act IV suggest a comparison of the triangle Rodogune–Nicanor–Antiochus with that of Chimène–Don Gomès–Rodrigue, but on the level of characterization it is little to the purpose. For in what social context can the murder of a future spouse to whom one's title is by no means clear create sanctions of the sort claimed by Rodogune? A demand for blood, tolerable in *Le Cid* for being carefully ritualized, would in the later play be merely savage, and we would be back where we started, with the incomprehensible Parthian. Recently Herland attempted to revive the thesis of vengeance for Nicanor with an interesting suggestion, the weaknesses of which he was himself the first to note, that Rodogune's Electra-like exhortations to Antiochus and Seleucus are literally what they seem to be figuratively, the voice of the murdered king's ghost, and therefore she is not morally responsible for them. Again, textual evidence is lacking. The ghost "spoke" once, but thereafter remained quiet, even though Rodogune quickly forgot her obligation. In retrospect, Herland's interpretation raises a question for every one that it answers, and the conclusion seems inescapable, that Rodogune's conduct in Act III, scene iv, has been forced on her by the dramatist. The only profitable question is, what did he expect to gain by the procedure to justify the inevitable obscurity?

That *Rodogune* held the stage as long as a purely rational dramaturgy was required only by a minority of the public, including professional critics like Boileau, whose theoretical concepts were in fact inadequate to analysis of plays of preceding decades, suggests that another method might better account for its history. The evolution in European art that progressively caused *Rodogune* to seem unnatural, until so characteristic an example of Corneille's theater virtually disappeared from repertory, is epitomized in the parallel destiny of critical terms that evolved antithetically, as it were, far from the original acceptation. While drama in 1644 tended toward a somewhat flat realism and no artist would gratuitously offend Nature or common sense, verisimilitude permitted a construction and a style that in modern theater is called expressionistic. That is, for the sake of sharper illumination, realism, especially diachronic, might be allowed to suffer, so that figural or symbolic patterns would be more clearly perceived. The major exigency of verisimilitude in Corneille's era seems to have been that characters in drama, for example, must respond naturally to one another, that is, naturally according to the laws of the world of that particular play. If a competent dramatist flouts this exigency, it must be for a strong reason.

The first step in solving the problem of Rodogune is to define the structural place or function of her role from act to act. In the exposition she is cast as protagonist-victim and therefore must be more virtuous than not. And since she will inevitably be overshadowed by her rival, Corneille had no choice but to make of her a tonal contrast. She appears at first fearful, uncertain, and almost gentle with all her pride—in short, vulnerable literally and figuratively. But the balance of the composition is altered at the first peripety. Rodogune's counter-thrust in retrospect seems to have been without function. In fact, it brings about a metastasis of structure: she is displaced from her post of protagonist-victim by Antiochus. That is, after Act III, scene iv, Rodogune becomes a quasi-object in Antiochus' world rather than a subject in her own. All her words are henceforth chosen for their effect on him, are directed only to him. As he displaces her, Antiochus divides the spectator's field of vision so that one sector is preempted by his own. That is, although the coherence of Rodogune's character is not salvable, the logic and consistency of her role can be discovered in the mind of the prince. For the crisis to

take the form Corneille has chosen, the spectator must be counted upon to follow the silent progress of Antiochus' thought: a natural resentment, constantly feeding on fear, might well have grown to murderous proportions. Though the spectator might experience some difficulty in taking the attack on Cleopatra seriously, he must allow that the princes are not wrong to do so. On the other hand, for suspicions to coexist with love, Antiochus must find Rodogune mysterious. He must hope, in short, that her actions possibly do not reflect a fundamentally evil character, such as he sees in Cleopatra, but he must be able to fear that they do. And the spectator must find Rodogune at least somewhat puzzling, to sympathize with Antiochus' disarray at the news of Seleucus' death. If Corneille stumbled, it is here. We forget that Antiochus has not seen Rodogune afraid and helpless. In his purview she is only harsh and strong-willed, and plausible motives for her extraordinary behavior are all too apparent. The royal palace of the Seleucids is no doubt a parable of the Louvre, and although the hypothesis that *Rodogune* was intended as a satire of the French court during the regency of Anne of Austria is hardly tenable, the broader parallel remains: life was fragile in Renaissance monarchies as it was in oriental kingdoms, and Corneille's spectator could easily credit the patent assumption that in the Syrian-Parthian context only one of the two heroines could survive. Antiochus can find them shocking, but their behavior appears more credible to him than it does to modern audiences, and it is consistent with *his* antecedent knowledge of them. His own conduct is then credible and consistent to the spectator. To this end Rodogune is designed for mystery as Cleopatra is for clarity. Rodogune is all appearance and no being, not because Corneille bungled the characterization, but in order that the projected pattern of the play might exist.[35]

The highest priority of Corneille's composition is the adjustment of Rodogune to Antiochus. Evidently the next in importance is the

---

35. Voltaire's cavil, ". . . it is a splendid touch, showing Antiochus in doubt and torn between mistress and mother, but unfortunately this beautiful situation could be created only at the expense of verisimilitude," seems plausible, for we too no longer respond appropriately to the figural rhetoric of Corneille's theater, and our efforts to save the surface verisimilitude obscure the dramatist's principal intention: to reveal the profound structure of personal interactions under stress. Voltaire's animadversions, however, contrarily suggest that one might better look for the allegorical sense of the whole play rather than demolish it in parts.

formal scheme of the tragedy. The unities as such are not in question here. The point is that *Rodogune* was constructed of symmetries, reflections, and echoes. Much of the mystery of the title-heroine would evaporate (and Herland's thesis be more convincing) if her soliloquy of Act III, scene iii, had been delivered in the first act, early enough for the vengeance motif to become a credible, essential part of the characterization. But Corneille did not in fact want to combine his *seconde Médée*[36] (that is, his Cleopatra) with a second Oresteia: he did intend that the third act faithfully mirror the second. Hence the soliloquy is placed precisely where it does the most damage to a kind of verisimilitude the dramatist is ready to forego. As with the characterization of Rodogune, so with almost every salient feature: hardly a one could withstand by itself the merciless tests to which the title-heroine has been subjected; but also, hardly a one can be singled out that does not prove to be a carefully placed element of the composition.

One of the most curious analyses of *Rodogune* to appear outside France came from Gotthold Lessing, who in the *Hamburgische Dramaturgie* attacked Corneille as the symbol of a bankrupt tradition. The essential quality of his plays, Lessing wrote,[37] is neither theatrical sorcery,[38] nor didactic idealism. They are comparable rather to a "kind of textile called *changeant*," that is, a cloth of which threads forming the warp are dyed a different color from the rest. From various angles one or the other color will predominate; agitation of the cloth itself dissolves them both in an iridescent shimmer. But if it is flattened and viewed in a precise right-angle perspective, they merge in dull confusion. So *Rodogune*, in Lessing's geometrically correct analysis, is everything a tragedy should not be. On the other hand, if his simile is exploited further, it can be turned against him: the ambiguities, the paradoxes, the flickering illumination, being essential, deliberate, are potent qualities and in no sense defects. Lessing, in fact, condemns all plays of this kind on moral grounds only. Like Voltaire[39] he shares the Rousseauistic prejudice that this

36. Author's *avertissement*, 1647.

37. In the "Dreißigstes Stück," 11 August 1767. See also articles 29, 31, and 32. August Wilhelm von Schlegel as well criticized *Rodogune* harshly in the Vienna lectures of 1808 on dramatic art (*Vorlesungen über dramatische Kunst und Literatur*, Leipzig, 1923).

38. See note 18 above and Borgerhoff, *Freedom of French Classicism*, pp. 55–56.

39. Lessing calls Corneille a bungler for not adhering to the simple, "natural"

kind of play, like *étoffe changeante*, can appeal only to an aristocratic and therefore unnatural, perverse, and ultimately immoral taste. But the general popularity as well as the critical praise accorded the *tragédie changeante* before 1650 suggests that it is not merely perverse to disagree with Voltaire and Lessing. Corneille's audience shared his conviction of the truth as well as beauty of such subjects. To satisfy the *esprits géométriques* of his era, he explains dutifully with every critical weapon in his arsenal such matters as Rodogune's puzzling behavior, but his mind is on the technical problems of maintaining the equilibrium between the rational mind that apprehends reality from but one perspective at a time, and the intuitive understanding that may comprehend a truth whole from multiple perspectives. He sought rather than avoided subjects to which material and ethical ambiguities are essential, and he reached his public with them because not even the average man of his century enjoyed the revolutionary faith that morality is self-evident and easy, or that perfect justice is a secular possibility. Before 1715 the contrary was an assumption so general that it was seldom stated explicitly. The point of *Rodogune*, one suspects, did not escape Lessing, but he did not like it any better than Voltaire would have done had the latter not missed it entirely. In the name of Progress both denied the dramatic system embodying what Corneille's era knew of man, a knowledge soon stifled in the rococo simplicity of expression they both preferred, and which above all cannot be manipulated to serve propagandistic goals such as they wrote their own plays to achieve. Corneille, undistracted by impulses to reform humanity *in toto*, purposes modestly to combine dramatic poses into figurative models embodying the integral human truth of complex situations, to build without myth or supernatural forces the actual traps of conflicting moral exigencies that catch even the strongest men—or better, especially the strongest—and wherein the only purely human tragedy lies.

It has been increasingly argued since the eighteenth century that the great majority of Corneille's tragedies are not in fact tragic and deserve rather the term attached in his era to a few of them: *comédie héroïque*. The thesis is debatable, especially in the extreme

---

scheme of Appian. Voltaire frequently complains in his edition of Corneille's theater that "ce qui n'est pas dans la nature ne peut toucher."

form Brunetière was the first, but not the last, to give it, inspired by a literary Darwinism still widely imitated. It is less easy to deal with the implications of L. Goldmann's criterion for serious drama, that interventions of chance not required by the "laws of the universe of that particular work" result in *drame*—meaning roughly, in this context, tragicomedy. By chance, it would seem, Antiochus and Rodogune have survived. R. Nelson, defining the world of *Rodogune* as half comic, half tragic, then denies tragic status to all characters but for Seleucus, with incontrovertible arguments, if questions of this kind can be decided by reducing a play to the sum of its characters' fates and their *sententiae*.[40] It is certain also that Corneille seldom represents to any dramatic purpose Freudian or existential *vertiges*, such as convulse Phèdre, or divinities such as would demand of Andromaque perjury and suicide, or a quasi-Proustian sense of time's corrosion such as suffuses the mind of Bérénice—in short, the Racinian hero's vulnerability to obsessive physical desires, paralysis of the will, or ineluctable destinies. Such facts and effects are inhibited by the nature of Corneille's universe: his humanity, in its total involvement, is not and cannot be subject to Romantic confusions of impulse or the nausea of impotence. If some of his protagonists appear passive at critical moments,[41] it is only where passivity is a form of ethical action, requiring, as we were once taught, the greatest tension of the will. And when they act, it is seldom a crime that, as crime, they make their own, as Phèdre makes incest her choice, as well as her destiny, by accusing the innocent Hippolyte of it to destroy him, since he will not share it. It is a truism that as a rule the Cornelian hero is undefeated. Whether that precludes tragedy is another question.

A point not often considered enough is that in the case of *Rodogune* the universe of the players has been shattered, and not by chance. Tragicomedies, like *comédies héroïques*, comedies and pastoral dramas, characteristically end with preservation and reconciliation. In Shakespearian tragedy, still accepted as such by the strict modern definition, it is even true that while men may be destroyed, mankind and nature are renewed before the final cadence. In Corneille, man often survives. But in *Rodogune* he survives in Cleopatra's world. To

---

40. Lucien Goldmann, *Jean Racine: dramaturge* (Paris, 1956), p. 13, and Nelson, *Corneille*, pp. 165 and 148
41. Argued by Léon Lemonnier, *Corneille* (Paris, 1945), and later by Herland.

perceive here Borgerhoff's tragic recognition, the "sudden awful revelation of what we are,"[42] we need only grant the classical premise that the measure of a life is its good, not its length. For Antiochus nothing is really settled but that he lives and will rule in Syria. But what kind of life remains? Without question the nascent idyll hinted at in the first act is blighted, for Cleopatra's ghost haunts the future. Her curse hangs in the air, and indeed, it may not be altogether far-fetched to imagine that Corneille meant the last lines as a compliment to those among his spectators who knew their Justin. After all, the historical Antiochus did have, not a child—the irony is even more appropriate—but a wife just like his mother.

TEXT AND TRANSLATION

The original edition of *Rodogune* was published in 1647; the last text corrected by the author himself appeared in the collective edition of 1682. Scherer employed the latter for his edition of *Rodogune* and his notes contain the variants of 1647. The present edition follows the text established by Ch. Marty-Laveaux in the *Grands Ecrivains de la France* collection, which reproduces the text of 1682, but with modern spelling and punctuation.[43] Like most successors to Marty-Laveaux, however, I have returned often to the punctuation of 1682, in which commas, for example, are used more freely to mark the manner in which lines are to be read. With this practice an occasional obscurity created by the nineteenth-century overly rationalized syntactical punctuation has been relieved.

Corneille employed in his great tragedies the sublime, characteristically chaste vocabulary and imagery of French neoclassicism. *Rodogune* has a poetry of its own, for the dramatist has returned to the baroque style of his earlier period, although he keeps it more firmly in hand. The contrapuntal arrangement of dramatic materials described above is echoed in paranomasia and polypton, antimetabole and anaphora (or epiphora), and especially in the logical figures of antithesis, oxymoron, paradox, irony, and syllepsis, the last named being a particularly characteristic figure of baroque French

---

42. *Freedom of French Classicism*, p. 72. In contrast, Herland and more recently Stegmann (*L'Héroïsme cornélien*, vol. 2, p. 452) allow that Corneille's art is authentically tragic. According to Stegmann the Cornelian hero acts in the name of a nontemporal order within a matrix of providential history.

43. Ch. Marty-Laveaux, ed., *Œuvres de Pierre Corneille*, 12 vols. (Paris, 1862–68).

drama.[44] Examples of each are noted in the text. It is sometimes objected that the frequency of such figures lends the Cornelian rhetoric a "cerebral," typically manneristic quality. Others, such as H. Hatzfeld, grant that in Corneille a "purer" baroque is often opposed to the mannerisms of writers of the third order.[45]

Be that as it may, Corneille's verse sets many problems for the translator. Prose is the medium chosen for this edition, since English, like most contemporary European languages, has almost lost the capacity for separation into the familiar, standard, and ceremonial levels of speech characteristic of the French of Corneille's era, and it has seemed best not to search for an equivalent of Corneille's *pompe*, an almost untranslatable word, but, roughly, the sublime in full-dress uniform. Its place is perhaps as well taken, and its absence compensated for, by rhythmic prose in which a natural vigor is aimed at, as by a more or less archaic vocabulary and heroic couplets or even blank verse. The following translation often departs, therefore, from the strict literal meaning of Corneille's text in the double aim of providing an English both natural and contemporary, without at the same time descending to triviality; and reproducing as faithfully as possible Corneille's rhetorical patterns, which are both more characteristic of his style than mere meter and lend more of the dramatic force for which he is supreme.

For the present edition and translation I am indebted to the staff of the Folger Library in Washington, D.C., and to those of the libraries of the Rutgers State University in New Brunswick, New Jersey, and of the University of California at Berkeley for their courtesy and innumerable services.

To Angela Merla Nuccitelli I owe special thanks for many kinds of aid in the preparation of the critical introduction and the translation.

WILLIAM G. CLUBB

---

44. Scherer, in *La dramaturgie classique* (above, n. 25), pp. 333–56, observes that *répétition* is the only figure significant to the analysis of his subject. Statistically that is true, but several other figures by the force they gain from place and function seem to be uniquely characteristic of this kind of drama.

45. Helmut Hatzfeld, *Estudios sobre el barroco* (Madrid, 1964), pp. 464–65, and p. 430, where Corneille's best plays, earlier criticized as *divertissements moraux*, are praised for relative purity of style. For *Rodogune* in particular and Corneille's return to the baroque luxuriance of *Clitandre*, see G. Couton, *Corneille et la Fronde* (Clermont-Ferrand, 1951), p. 17.

RODOGUNE

ACTEURS

CLÉOPÂTRE, reine de Syrie, veuve de Démétrius Nicanor

SÉLEUCUS
ANTIOCHUS } fils de Démétrius et de Cléopâtre

RODOGUNE, sœur de Phraates, Roi des Parthes

TIMAGÈNE, gouverneur des deux Princes

ORONTE, ambassadeur de Phraates

LAONICE, sœur de Timagène, confidente de Cléopâtre

La scène est à Séleucie, dans le palais royal.

DRAMATIS PERSONAE

CLEOPATRA, Queen of Syria, widow of Demetrius Nicanor
SELEUCUS ⎫
ANTIOCHUS⎭sons of Demetrius and Cleopatra
RODOGUNE, sister of Phraates, king of Parthia
TIMAGENES, tutor to the two princes
ORONTES, the ambassador of Phraates
LAONICE, sister of Timagenes, Cleopatra's confidante

The setting is the royal palace in Seleucia.

Rodogune
Princesse des Parthes
Tragedie

ACTE I

Laonice *et* Timagène.

LAONICE.
   Enfin ce jour pompeux, cet heureux jour nous luit,
   Qui d'un trouble si long doit dissiper la nuit,
   Ce grand jour où l'hymen, étouffant la vengeance,
   Entre le Parthe et nous remet l'intelligence,
   Affranchit sa princesse, et nous fait pour jamais   5
   Du motif de la guerre un lien de la paix.
   Ce grand jour est venu, mon frère, où notre reine,
   Cessant de plus tenir la couronne incertaine,
   Doit rompre aux yeux de tous son silence obstiné,
   De deux princes gémeaux nous déclarer l'aîné;   10
   Et l'avantage seul d'un moment de naissance,
   Dont elle a jusqu'ici caché la connaissance,
   Mettant au plus heureux le sceptre dans la main,
   Va faire l'un sujet, et l'autre souverain.
   Mais n'admirez-vous point que cette même reine   15
   Le donne pour époux à l'objet de sa haine,
   Et n'en doit faire un roi qu'afin de couronner
   Celle que dans les fers elle aimait à gêner?
   Rodogune, par elle en esclave traitée,
   Par elle se va voir sur le trône montée,   20
   Puisque celui des deux qu'elle nommera roi
   Lui doit donner la main et recevoir sa foi.
TIMAGÈNE.
   Pour le mieux admirer, trouver bon, je vous prie,
   Que j'apprenne de vous les troubles de Syrie.
   J'en ai vu les premiers, et me souviens encor   25

The Tragedy of Rodogune

Princess of Parthia

ACT I

[I.i]   Laonice *and* Timagenes.

LAONICE.

At last with this great ceremony the long night of bitter
strife has passed; at last the glorious wedding day breaks to
still the tongue of vengeance. With the Parthian we speak
again; their princess is free and yesterday's cause of war
is today's bond of peace. Our great day, brother, has come;
the queen must break her stubborn silence and end the
doubt where the crown must be worn; she must declare to
us all the elder of the two princes, and the moment's advantage bringing one to the world before the other, the secret so
long hidden from us, she must reveal now; and as she
bestows the scepter one becomes sovereign, the other his
subject. But do you not wonder, that this very queen gives
her son as husband to a hated rival and creates a king only
to crown the woman she delighted to torture in irons?
Rodogune, whom she treated like her slave, is by her
desire to ascend the throne; for whoever is named king
must give her his hand and be sworn her faith.

TIMAGENES.

So that I may wonder still more, tell me, if you will, your
story of Syria's troubles. I saw the first of them and

Des malheureux succès du grand roi Nicanor,
Quand des Parthes vaincus pressant l'adroite fuite
Il tomba dans leur fers au bout de sa poursuite.
Je n'ai pas oublié que cet événement
Du perfide Tryphon fit le soulèvement.   30
Voyant le Roi captif, la Reine désolée,
Il crut pouvoir saisir la couronne ébranlée;
Et le sort, favorable à son lâche attentat,
Mit d'abord sous ses lois la moitié de l'État.
La Reine, craignant tout de ces nouveaux orages,   35
En sut mettre à l'abri ses plus précieux gages;
Et pour n'exposer pas l'enfance de ses fils,
Me les fit chez son frère enlever à Memphis.
Là, nous n'avons rien su que de la renommée,
Qui par un bruit confus diversement semée,   40
N'a porté jusqu'à nous ces grands renversements
Que sous l'obscurité de cent déguisements.

LAONICE.

Sachez donc que Tryphon après quatre batailles
Ayant su nous réduire à ces seules murailles,
En forma tôt le siège, et pour comble d'effroi,   45
Un faux bruit s'y coula touchant la mort du Roi.
Le peuple épouvanté, qui déjà dans son âme
Ne suivait qu'à regret les ordres d'une femme,
Voulut forcer la Reine à choisir un époux.
Que pouvait-elle faire et seule et contre tous?   50
Croyant son mari mort, elle épousa son frère.
L'effet montra soudain ce conseil salutaire;
Le prince Antiochus devenu nouveau Roi
Sembla de tous côtés traîner l'heur avec soi:
La victoire attachée au progrès de ses armes   55
Sur nos fiers ennemis rejeta nos alarmes,
Et la mort de Tryphon dans un dernier combat,
Changeant tout notre sort, lui rendit tout l'État.
Quelque promesse alors qu'il eût faite à la mère
De remettre ses fils au trône de leur père,   60
Il témoigna si peu de la vouloir tenir,
Qu'elle n'osa jamais les faire revenir.
Ayant régné sept ans, son ardeur militaire
Ralluma cette guerre où succomba son frère,

remember great Nicanor's misfortune when, pressing hard
after the defeated Parthians in their crafty retreat, he fell
still pursuing into their hands; nor do I forget how this
disaster led to the rebellion of perfidious Tryphon. Seeing
the king in captivity, the queen alone and helpless, he
thought he could seize the unsteady throne; and Fortune
favoring his cowardly assault, at one stroke brought half
the nation under his rule. The queen, in fear that she
would lose everything in these new storms, was able at least
to send the princes to safety; so that in their infancy they
might not be exposed to such peril, she had me take them
to Memphis, to her brother's court. There we learned
nothing of these great calamities but rumor, which brought
them to us, but as if in a babel of tongues, obscured in
hundredfold disguise.

LAONICE.

You must know then that after four battles Tryphon drove
us within these walls and soon laid siege. And, raising our
fear to its height, false rumors were spread about the death
of the king. The terrified populace, already loath in their
hearts to suffer a woman's command, forced her to choose a
suitor. Alone and against them all, what could she do? In
the belief her husband was dead, she became his brother's
wife. Events soon showed this course to be the safest. At
every turn, Fortune showered her favors on prince
Antiochus, now king; wherever he bore his arms Victory
smiled; and the terrors that had shaken us she allotted to
our fierce enemy. In a last struggle, Tryphon's death
changed all our destiny and restored to Antiochus a
united kingdom. Then despite all promises to the mother
that he would restore their father's throne to her sons, he
showed such little mind to keep his word that she dared not
recall them to her side. After reigning seven years his
martial fever rekindled the very war in which the brother
had fallen. He attacked the Parthians, and confident of his

Il attaqua le Parthe, et se crut assez fort   65
Pour en venger sur lui la prison, et la mort.
Jusque dans ses États il lui porta la guerre,
Il s'y fit partout craindre à l'égal du tonnerre,
Il lui donna bataille, où mille beaux exploits. . . .
Je vous achèverai le reste une autre fois,   70
Un des princes survient.   *Elle se veut retirer.*

[I.ii]   *Les mêmes*, Antiochus.

ANTIOCHUS.   Demeurez, Laonice,
Vous pouvez, comme lui, me rendre un bon office.
Dans l'état où je suis, triste et plein de souci,
Si j'espère beaucoup, je crains beaucoup aussi.
Un seul mot aujourd'hui maître de ma fortune   75
M'ôte, ou donne à jamais le sceptre, et Rodogune,
Et de tous les mortels ce secret révélé
Me rend le plus content ou le plus désolé.
Je vois dans le hasard tous les biens que j'espère,
Et ne puis être heureux sans le malheur d'un frère;   80
Mais d'un frère si cher, qu'une sainte amitié
Fait sur moi de ses maux rejaillir la moitié.
Donc pour moins hasarder j'aime mieux moins prétendre,
Et pour rompre le coup que mon cœur n'ose attendre,
Lui cédant de deux biens le plus brillant aux yeux,   85
M'assurer de celui qui m'est plus précieux.
Heureux, si sans attendre un fâcheux droit d'aînesse
Pour un trône incertain j'en obtiens la Princesse,
Et puis par ce partage épargner les soupirs
Qui naîtraient de ma peine, ou de ses déplaisirs.   90
    Va le voir de ma part, Timagène, et lui dire
Que pour cette beauté je lui céde l'empire;
Mais porte-lui si haut la douceur de régner,
Qu'à cet éclat du trône il se laisse gagner,
Qu'il s'en laisse éblouir, jusqu'à ne pas connaître   95
A quel prix je consens de l'accepter pour maître.

Timagène *s'en va, et le Prince continue à parler à* Laonice.

    Et vous, en ma faveur voyez ce cher objet,
Et tâchez d'abaisser ses yeux sur un sujet

power, meant to avenge his brother's captivity and death. He carried the war into their own states, feared everywhere more than the thunderbolt, for in those battles a thousand glorious deeds— But one of the princes is coming to us. I shall tell you the rest another time.

She prepares to withdraw.

[I.ii]   *Enter* Antiochus.

ANTIOCHUS.

Stay, Laonice, for you may both be able to do me service.

In this wretched state, sad and heavy with cares, if my hopes rise high, my fear looms as large. A single word today decides my fate; a single word can forever give or wrest from me the scepter and Rodogune. When the secret is out I am the happiest or most wretched mortal alive. All that I prize, all my hopes I see in jeopardy; I cannot be fortunate but in a brother's misfortune, and he a brother so close, bound by love so sacred that half his pains recoil on me. And so, to diminish the risk I would ask for less; to prevent the thrust my heart cannot withstand I would surrender to him the more brilliant reward and secure for myself the more precious, happy if waiting no longer to learn of the first-born's unwelcome priority, I have the princess instead of an uncertain throne; and happy if by sharing we are spared the anguish of my pain or his sorrows.

In my name, go see him, Timagenes, and tell him that for Rodogune's beauty I leave him the empire; but praise so highly the sweet joys of power that the throne's dazzle shall blind him to the cost, to the reward for which I willingly accept his rule.

Timagenes *exits, and the Prince continues to talk with* Laonice.

And you, go to my dear love, press her to look with favor

Qui peut-être aujourd'hui porterait la couronne,
S'il n'attachait les siens à sa seule personne,   100
Et ne la préférait à cet illustre rang
Pour qui les plus grands cœurs prodiguent tout leur sang.

              Timagène *rentre sur le théâtre.*

TIMAGÈNE

Seigneur, le Prince vient, et votre amour lui-même
Lui peut sans interprète offrir le diadème.

ANTIOCHUS.

Ah! je tremble, et la peur d'un trop juste refus   105
Rend ma langue muette, et mon esprit confus.

[I.iii]   *Les mêmes,* Séleucus.

SÉLEUCUS.

Vous puis-je en confiance expliquer ma pensée?

ANTIOCHUS.

Parlez, notre amitié par ce doute est blessée.

SÉLEUCUS.

Hélas! c'est le malheur que je crains aujourd'hui.
L'égalité, mon frère, en est le ferme appui,   110
C'en est le fondement, la liaison, le gage,
Et voyant d'un côté tomber tout l'avantage,
Avec juste raison je crains qu'entre nous deux
L'égalité rompue en rompe les doux nœuds,
Et que ce jour fatal à l'heur de notre vie   115
Jette sur l'un de nous trop de honte, ou d'envie.

ANTIOCHUS.

Comme nous n'avons eu jamais qu'un sentiment,
Cette peur me touchait, mon frère, également,
Mais si vous le voulez, j'en sais bien le remède.

SÉLEUCUS.

Si je le veux! bien plus, je l'apporte, et vous cède   120
Tout ce que la couronne a de charmant en soi.
Oui, Seigneur, car je parle à présent à mon roi,
Pour le trône cédé cédez-moi Rodogune,
Et je n'envierai point votre haute fortune.
Ainsi notre destin n'aura rien de honteux,   125
Ainsi notre bonheur n'aura rien de douteux,

on her subject, who might wear a crown but that his eyes
are fixed on her alone, whose person he treasures more than
that illustrious rank for which the noblest hearts have shed
their prodigal blood.

Timagenes *re-enters.*

TIMAGENES.

My lord, the prince is coming here, and your heart may do
its own embassy, offering him the diadem.

ANTIOCHUS.

Ah, I tremble for fear of an all too just refusal! My mind is
in turmoil, my tongue is stilled.

[I.iii]   *Enter* Seleucus.

SELEUCUS.

May I open my mind to you in good faith?

ANTIOCHUS.

Of course you may; to doubt it is to offend our affection.

SELEUCUS.

Ah, that is the misfortune I fear today. Equality, brother,
is the soil that sustains it, nourishes it, preserves it. But if
one should see every advantage fall to the other, I fear, and
with good reason, the broken balance must break our ties;
for this day must be fatal to our happiness, casting on one
alone too much shame or envy.

ANTIOCHUS.

As we have ever felt as one, that fear oppresses me as much.
But if you will agree, I know a remedy.

SELEUCUS.

I will agree, of course! Moreover, I have one of my own.
I surrender the crown with all its glory. Yes, sire, for now I
speak to my king; and for the throne surrendered, surrender to me Rodogune. Never will I envy your high destiny.
Then our fate will bring no shame, then our happiness will
not be clouded with doubts, and despite feeble claims to the

Et nous mépriserons ce faible droit d'aînesse,
Vous, satisfait du trône, et moi, de la Princesse.

ANTIOCHUS.

Hélas!

SÉLEUCUS. Recevez-vous l'offre avec déplaisir?

ANTIOCHUS.

Pouvez-vous nommer offre une ardeur de choisir,   130
Qui de la même main qui me cède un empire
M'arrache un bien plus grand, et le seul où j'aspire?

SÉLEUCUS.

Rodogune?

ANTIOCHUS.   Elle-même, ils en sont les témoins.

SÉLEUCUS.

Quoi? l'estimez-vous tant?

ANTIOCHUS.   Quoi? l'estimez-vous moins?

SÉLEUCUS.

Elle vaut bien un trône, il faut que je le die.   135

ANTIOCHUS.

Elle vaut à mes yeux tout ce qu'en a l'Asie.

SÉLEUCUS.

Vous l'aimez donc, mon frère?

ANTIOCHUS.   Et vous l'aimez aussi;
C'est là tout mon malheur, c'est là tout mon souci.
J'espérais que l'éclat dont le trône se pare
Toucherait vos désirs plus qu'un objet si rare,   140
Mais aussi bien qu'à moi son prix vous est connu,
Et dans ce juste choix vous m'avez prévenu.
Ah, déplorable prince!

SÉLEUCUS.   Ah, destin trop contraire!

ANTIOCHUS.

Que ne ferais-je point contre un autre qu'un frère?

SÉLEUCUS.

O mon cher frère! O nom pour un rival trop doux!   145
Que ne ferais-je point contre un autre que vous?

ANTIOCHUS.

Où nous vas-tu réduire, amitié fraternelle?

right of prior birth, you shall be content with the crown, I
in the love of the princess.

ANTIOCHUS.

Oh, my brother!

SELEUCUS.

Does my offer displease you?

ANTIOCHUS.

Is it an offer, when with one hand you give me an empire
and with the other rob me of a richer treasure, the only one
I long to possess?

SELEUCUS.

Rodogune?

ANTIOCHUS.

Rodogune herself, as they can testify.

[*Indicates* Laonice *and* Timagenes.]

SELEUCUS.

What? Is she all that to you?

ANTIOCHUS.

And is she any less to you?

SELEUCUS.

It must be said, I prize her no less than the throne.

ANTIOCHUS.

In my eyes, she is more than all the thrones of Asia.

SELEUCUS.

You love her then, brother?

ANTIOCHUS.

And you love her too. Ah, for that only am I unfortunate,
for that only I must grieve. I hoped the throne and its
glory might move you more than Rodogune's rare beauty;
but for you as for me she is the prize, and your choice must
forestall mine. Can a prince be more pitiable?

SELEUCUS.

Can fate be more contrary?

ANTIOCHUS.

What would I not attempt against anyone but a brother?

SELEUCUS.

Oh, my brother—rival is too harsh a word—what would I
not attempt against anyone but you?

ANTIOCHUS.

To what are we reduced by a brother's love?

SÉLEUCUS.

Amour, qui doit ici vaincre de vous, ou d'elle ?

ANTIOCHUS.

L'amour, l'amour doit vaincre, et la triste amitié
Ne doit être à tous deux qu'un objet de pitié.   150
Un grand cœur cède un trône, et le cède avec gloire,
Cet effort de vertu couronne sa mémoire ;
Mais lorsqu'un digne objet a pu nous enflammer,
Qui le cède est un lâche et ne sait pas aimer.
De tous deux Rodogune a charmé le courage,   155
Cessons par trop d'amour de lui faire un outrage.
Elle doit épouser, non pas vous, non pas moi,
Mais de moi, mais de vous, quiconque sera roi :
La couronne entre nous flotte encore incertaine,
Mais sans incertitude elle doit être reine ;   160
Cependant, aveuglés dans notre vain projet,
Nous la faisions tous deux la femme d'un sujet !
Régnons, l'ambition ne peut être que belle,
Et pour elle quittée, et reprise pour elle,
Et ce trône, où tous deux nous osions renoncer,   165
Souhaitons-le tous deux, afin de l'y placer.
C'est dans notre destin le seul conseil à prendre,
Nous pouvons nous en plaindre, et nous devons l'attendre.

SÉLEUCUS.

Il faut encor plus faire, il faut qu'en ce grand jour
Notre amitié triomphe aussi bien que l'amour.   170
Ces deux sièges fameux de Thèbes, et de Troie,
Qui mirent l'une en sang, l'autre aux flammes en proie,
N'eurent pour fondements à leurs maux infinis,
Que ceux que contre nous le sort a réunis.
Il sème entre nous deux toute la jalousie   175
Qui dépeupla la Grèce, et saccagea l'Asie ;
Un même espoir du sceptre est permis à tous deux,
Pour la même beauté nous faisons mêmes vœux ;
Thèbes périt pour l'un, Troie a brûlé pour l'autre,
Tout va choir en ma main, ou tomber en la vôtre,   180
En vain notre amitié tâchait à partager,
Et si j'ose tout dire, un titre assez léger,
Un droit d'aînesse obscur, sur la foi d'une mère,
Va combler l'un de gloire, et l'autre de misère.

SELEUCUS.

Must love prove stronger, or a brother's affection?

ANTIOCHUS.

Love, love must conquer; and our wretched affection
should move the victor only to pity. A nobler heart will
give up the throne and gain a greater fame, and his virtuous effort will crown his memory; but when our love
burns for a worthy object, whoever would surrender it is
love's coward, knows not how to love.

Rodogune has cast her spell on both our hearts. Let us
not do her an outrage from too great a love. She must wed
not you, not me, but, whether it be I or you, the king. The
crown floats between us, uncertain still, but certain it is,
she must be queen. And all this time, in our blind desire, in
our vanity, we dreamed she might be wife to a mere vassal?
Let us reign; royal ambition can be glorious only if aban-
doned or embraced for her. And this throne, that both had
courage to renounce, let both covet it, so that on it we may
place Rodogune. Our fate can resolve us only to this; complain as we will, we must expect no more.

SELEUCUS.

There is a still greater deed; victorious on this great day as
lovers, so must we be as brothers.

The oft-sung wars of Thebes and Troy, drowning one in
blood, destroying the other in flames, had their roots in the
very same evils Fate has set in our path. In us it has sown
seeds of the very jealousy that unpeopled the lands of
Greece, that put Asia to the sword; the hope of one scepter
is given to both, both our hearts are set on one beauty!
Thebes perished for the first cause, Troy fell for the
second. Here, everything must come to my hand, or to
yours. In vain the love of brother for brother would share
equally, and—dare I say it all?—a slight claim, an uncertain priority, that depends on a mother's word, must exalt

Que de sujets de plainte en ce double intérêt 185
Aura le malheureux contre un si faible arrêt!
Que de sources de haine! Hélas, jugez le reste;
Craignez-en avec moi l'événement funeste,
Ou plutôt avec moi faites un digne effort
Pour armer votre cœur contre un si triste sort. 190
Malgré l'éclat du trône, et l'amour d'une femme,
Faisons si bien régner l'amitié sur notre âme,
Qu'étouffant dans leur perte un regret suborneur,
Dans le bonheur d'un frère on trouve son bonheur.
Ainsi ce qui jadis perdit Thèbes, et Troie 195
Dans nos cœurs mieux unis ne versera que joie,
Ainsi notre amitié triomphante à son tour
Vaincra la jalousie, en cédant à l'amour,
Et de notre destin bravant l'ordre barbare
Trouvera des douceurs aux maux qu'il nous prépare. 200

ANTIOCHUS.

Le pourrez-vous, mon frère?

SÉLEUCUS.   Ah, que vous me pressez!
Je le voudrai du moins, mon frère, et c'est assez.
Et ma raison sur moi gardera tant d'empire,
Que je désavouerai mon cœur, s'il en soupire.

ANTIOCHUS.

J'embrasse comme vous ces nobles sentiments. 205
Mais allons leur donner le secours des serments,
Afin, qu'étant témoins de l'amitié jurée,
Les Dieux contre un tel coup assurent sa durée.

SÉLEUCUS.

Allons, allons l'étreindre au pied de leurs autels
Par des liens sacrés et des nœuds immortels. 210

[I.iv]   Laonice *et* Timagène.

LAONICE.

Peut-on plus dignement mériter la couronne?

TIMAGÈNE.

Je ne suis point surpris de ce qui vous étonne;
Confident de tous deux, prévoyant leur douleur,
J'ai prévu leur constance, et j'ai plaint leur malheur.
Mais de grâce, achevez l'historie commencée. 215

one of us and fill the other with grief. See how many accusations the unfortunate one can lay against such a feeble authority! How many reasons to hate! And weigh what must follow: we must both fear the mortal consequence. But instead, let us stand nobly, let us be armed against these evil days. Despite the glory of a throne, the powers of love, let our hearts be so ruled by affection that no regret can corrupt them, and in the loss find happiness in a brother's good fortune. Then the source of Theban and Trojan disasters will unite us in joy; then our affection will be victorious, conquering jealousy in surrender to love. In defiance of our barbarous destiny, happiness will be found in the evils it has decreed.

ANTIOCHUS.

Will that be possible for you?

SELEUCUS.

Oh, the question oppresses me! I shall wish it so, at least, and that is enough. My mind shall so command my heart, I will disown it, if it but sigh.

ANTIOCHUS.

Like you, I will embrace these noble sentiments, but let us add the strength of solemn vows, so the Gods in witness of our sworn affection may let it endure through these trials.

SELEUCUS.

Come, let us make holy the bonds of our love, swearing at the altar to our undying faith.

Exeunt Antiochus *and* Seleucus.

[I.iv]   Laonice *and* Timagenes.

LAONICE.

Can heirs to a crown be nobler than these?

TIMAGENES.

What astonishes you is no surprise to me. Both have confided their passion to me, and foreseeing their sorrow, I foresaw they would stand firm; and I feel their misfortune deeply. But, if you will, relate the end of the story you began.

LAONICE.

Pour la reprendre donc où nous l'avons laissée,
Les Parthes au combat par les nôtres forcés,
Tantôt presque vainqueurs, tantôt presque enfoncés,
Sur l'une et l'autre armée également heureuse
Virent longtemps voler la victoire douteuse;   220
Mais la fortune enfin se tourna contra nous,
Si bien qu'Antiochus percé de mille coups,
Près de tomber aux mains d'une troupe ennemie
Lui voulut dérober les restes de sa vie,
Et préférant aux fers la gloire de périr,   225
Lui-même par sa main acheva de mourir.
La Reine, ayant appris cette triste nouvelle,
En reçut tôt après une autre plus cruelle,
Que Nicanor vivait, que sur un faux rapport
De ce premier époux elle avait cru la mort,   230
Que piqué jusqu'au vif contre son hyménée
Son âme à l'imiter s'était déterminée,
Et que, pour s'affranchir des fers de son vainqueur,
Il allait épouser la Princesse sa sœur.
C'est cette Rodogune, où l'un et l'autre frère   235
Trouve encor les appas qu'avait trouvés leur père.
La Reine envoie en vain pour se justifier,
On a beau la défendre, on a beau le prier,
On ne rencontre en lui qu'un juge inexorable,
Et son amour nouveau la veut croire coupable;   240
Son erreur est un crime, et pour l'en punir mieux,
Il veut même épouser Rodogune à ses yeux,
Arracher de son front le sacré diadème,
Pour ceindre une autre tête en sa présence même;
Soit qu'ainsi sa vengeance eût plus d'indignité,   245
Soit qu'ainsi cet hymen eût plus d'autorité,
Et qu'il assurât mieux par cette barbarie,
Aux enfants qui naîtraient le trône de Syrie.
Mais tandis qu'animé de colère, et d'amour
Il vient déshériter ses fils par son retour,   250
Et qu'un gros escadron de Parthes pleins de joie
Conduit ces deux amants et court comme à la proie,
La Reine au désespoir de n'en rien obtenir,
Se résout de le perdre, ou de le prévenir.

LAONICE.

To go on from where we stopped: the Parthians were forced
to battle by our soldiers; and sometimes almost victorious,
sometimes almost defeated, they saw their doubtful victory
fly from each army in turn, until at last Fortune frowned
on ours. Antiochus, bleeding from a thousand wounds, was
about to fall into enemy hands. But to breathe his last in
freedom, wanting to die in glory rather than be captured,
he with his own hand dealt the mortal blow. Following
hard on this grievous news, there came to the queen another
more bitter still: Nicanor was alive, and she had thought
him dead on a false report. Pierced to the quick by her
marriage, he had resolved to take example by her. To
shake off his prisoner's chains he was ready to marry his
royal captor's sister, the princess Rodogune, the same who
before our two princes had first charmed their father. The
queen sued for pardon, but in vain. No plea, no defense
was allowed. To all embassies he turned an inexorable face;
his new passion heard only her guilt. The error was a
crime, and the better to punish her, he would even wed
Rodogune before her very eyes, wrest the sacred diadem
from her brow, and in her very presence set it upon
another's. Perhaps it was a greater authority he wanted
for this marriage, or greater humiliation in his vengeance,
or perhaps he gained greater assurance by this barbarous
action that the children to be born would inherit Syria's
crown.

Thus aflame with anger, and love, Nicanor returns to
disinherit his sons, guarded by a large troop of exultant
Parthians eager to escort the royal couple as if in pursuit of
their prey. The queen, in despair that her envoys had
gained no favor, is resolved to forestall him, or lose all in

Elle oublie un mari qui veut cesser de l'être, 255
Qui ne veut plus la voir qu'en implacable maître,
Et changeant à regret son amour en horreur,
Elle abandonne tout à sa juste fureur.
Elle-même leur dresse une embûche au passage,
Se mêle dans les coups, porte partout sa rage, 260
En pousse jusqu'au bout les furieux effets.
Que vous dirai-je enfin ? les Parthes sont défaits,
Le Roi meurt, et, dit-on, par la main de la Reine.
Rodogune captive est livrée à sa haine ;
Tous les maux qu'un esclave endure dans les fers, 265
Alors sans moi, mon frère, elle les eût soufferts ;
La Reine à la gêner prenant mille délices
Ne commettait qu'à moi l'ordre de ses supplices ;
Mais quoi que m'ordonnât cette âme toute en feu,
Je promettais beaucoup et j'exécutais peu. 270
Le Parthe cependant en jure la vengeance,
Sur nous à main armée il fond en diligence,
Nous surprend, nous assiège, et fait un tel effort,
Que la ville aux abois, on lui parle d'accord.
Il veut fermer l'oreille, enflé de l'avantage, 275
Mais voyant parmi nous Rodogune en otage,
Enfin il craint pour elle, et nous daigne écouter,
Et c'est ce qu'aujourd'hui l'on doit exécuter.
 La Reine de l'Égypte a rappelé nos princes,
Pour remettre à l'aîné son trône, et ses provinces, 280
Rodogune a paru sortant de sa prison,
Comme un soleil levant dessus notre horizon,
Le Parthe a décampé pressé par d'autres guerres
Contre l'Arménien qui ravage ses terres ;
D'un ennemi cruel il s'est fait notre appui, 285
La paix finit la haine, et pour comble aujourd'hui,
Dois-je dire bonne, ou mauvaise fortune ?
Nos deux princes tous deux adorent Rodogune.

TIMAGÈNE.

Sitôt qu'ils ont paru tous deux en cette cour,
Ils ont vu Rodogune, et j'ai vu leur amour : 290
Mais comme étant rivaux nous les trouvons à plaindre,
Connaissant leur vertu, je n'en vois rien à craindre.
Pour vous qui gouvernez cet objet de leurs vœux—

the attempt. She forgets this husband who would deny the name and see her no more but as her implacable master. Love she changes, with regret, to horror; she spares nothing in her just fury. She herself waits for them in ambush, she strikes about, raging everywhere, fury driven to its height. What more is there to tell? In the Parthian rout the king died, they say, by the queen's own hand, and left Rodogune captive, helpless before her hatred. All that a manacled slave endures she would then have suffered but for me. The queen delighted endlessly in tormenting her, but she trusted me alone to torture at her behest. Yet, whatever the commands of that soul on fire, I promised much, I obeyed little. Meanwhile the Parthians swore vengeance; in rapid armed advance they fall on us, they besiege us, and to such effect that with the city at bay, the queen must sue for truce. Swollen in their might, they would turn deaf ears, but with Rodogune our hostage, they must fear us; perforce they deign to listen; so today we execute the treaty.

The queen has called her sons home from Egypt, restoring to the elder both throne and state; Rodogune has come forth from prison, shining like the new sun on our horizon. The Parthians have broken camp and gone to war against the Armenians, who lay waste their lands. The cruel foe has become an ally, and peace ends our hatred; the crown of our fortune—or should it be called good or evil chance—is that both our princes adore Rodogune.

TIMAGENES.

No sooner did they appear at court than they saw Rodogune, and I saw they loved her; and though as rivals we must pity them, knowing their virtue I see no cause for fear. And you, who have charge of the one they love—

LAONICE.

Et n'ai point encor vu qu'elle aime aucun des deux.

TIMAGÈNE.

Vous me trouvez mal propre à cette confidence,   295
Et peut-être à dessein je la vois qui s'avance.
Adieu, je dois au rang qu'elle est prête à tenir
Du moins la liberté de vous entretenir.   [*Exit.*]

[I.v]   Rodogune *et* Laonice.

RODOGUNE.

Je ne sais quel malheur aujourd'hui me menace,
Et coule dans ma joie une secrète glace,   300
Je tremble, Laonice, et te voulais parler,
Ou pour chasser ma crainte, ou pour m'en consoler.

LAONICE.

Quoi, Madame, en ce jour pour vous si plein de gloire?

RODOGUNE.

Ce jour m'en promet tant, que j'ai peine à tout croire.
La fortune me traite avec trop de respect,   305
Et le trône, et l'hymen, tout me devient suspect.
L'hymen semble à mes yeux cacher quelque supplice,
Le trône, sous mes pas creuser un précipice,
Je vois de nouveaux fers après les miens brisés,
Et je prends tous ces biens pour des maux déguisés.   310
En un mot, je crains tout de l'esprit de la Reine.

LAONICE.

La paix qu'elle a jurée en a calmé la haine.

RODOGUNE.

La haine entre les grands se calme rarement,
La paix souvent n'y sert que d'un amusement,
Et dans l'état où j'entre, à te parler sans feinte,   315
Elle a lieu de me craindre, et je crains cette crainte.
Non qu'enfin je ne donne au bien des deux États
Ce que j'ai dû de haine à de tels attentats,
J'oublie, et pleinement, toute mon aventure:
Mais une grande offense est de cette nature,   320
Que toujours son auteur impute à l'offensé
Un vif ressentiment dont il le croit blessé,
Et quoiqu'en apparence on les réconcilie,

LAONICE.

And still do not see that she loves either—

TIMAGENES.

You do not see fit to entrust me with her secrets. Indeed, there she comes, perhaps intending to speak with you. Farewell, I owe the rank she is about to assume at least the freedom to converse with you as she will.

Exit Timagenes.

[I.v]   *Enter* Rodogune.

RODOGUNE.

I cannot tell what evil threatens today and freezes the joy in my heart. Why do I tremble, Laonice? Have I sought you out in hopes my fear may melt away, or do I hope in speaking to be consoled?

LAONICE.

What, madam, today, the very day of your glory?

RODOGUNE.

This day is too full of promises; I can scarce believe them all. Fortune wears a face too kind. Both throne and wedding, everything stirs my doubt. Behind the wedding I seem to glimpse new torment; the throne suspends me over an abyss. I see new chains in wait, now the old are broken. Every joy seems to me a mask of evil. To say it and have done, I fear every impulse of the queen's heart.

LAONICE.

The treaty she has sworn stills her hatred.

RODOGUNE.

The hatred of great houses is seldom stilled, and peace is often but a snare. The high rank I assume today, in naked truth, is a reason for her to have fear of me—and I am afraid of that fear. Not that I will not sacrifice the hatred I owed her for my sufferings to the welfare of our nations. I willingly forget, fully, all the past. But it is in the nature of · great offenses that the offender assumes his victim must harbor a violent spite; he cannot believe the wound is forgotten. And though they might seem reconciled, he is

Il le craint, il le hait, et jamais ne s'y fie,
Et toujours alarmé de cette illusion, 325
Sitôt qu'il peut le perdre, il prend l'occasion.
Telle est pour moi la Reine.

LAONICE.   Ah, Madame, je jure
Que par ce faux soupçon vous lui faites injure.
Vous devez oublier un désespoir jaloux,
Où força son courage un infidèle époux. 330
Si teinte de son sang, et toute furieuse
Elle vous traita lors en rivale odieuse,
L'impétuosité d'un premier mouvement
Engageait sa vengeance à ce dur traitement;
Il fallait un prétexte à vaincre sa colère, 335
Il y fallait du temps, et pour ne vous rien taire,
Quand je me dispensais à lui mal obéir,
Quand en votre faveur je semblais la trahir,
Peut-être qu'en son cœur plus douce, et repentie,
Elle en dissimulait la meilleure partie, 340
Que se voyant tromper elle fermait les yeux,
Et qu'un peu de pitié la satisfaisait mieux.
A présent que l'amour succède à la colère,
Elle ne vous voit plus qu'avec des yeux de mère,
Et si de cet amour je la voyais sortir, 345
Je jure de nouveau de vous en avertir.
Vous savez comme quoi je vous suis toute acquise:
Le Roi souffrirait-il d'ailleurs quelque surprise?

RODOGUNE.
Qui que ce soit des deux, qu'on couronne aujourd'hui,
Elle sera mère, et pourra tout sur lui. 350

LAONICE.
Qui que ce soit des deux, je sais qu'il vous adore.
Connaissant leur amour, pouvez-vous craindre encore?

RODOGUNE.
Oui, je crains leur hymen, et d'être à l'un des deux.

LAONICE.
Quoi, sont-ils des sujets indignes de vos feux?

RODOGUNE.
Comme ils ont même sang avec pareil mérite, 355
Un avantage égal pour eux me sollicite,
Mais il est malaisé dans cette égalité

afraid; and fear breeding hatred, he can never rest, never
trust; and constantly alarmed by his delusion, he will destroy the other at the first chance. That is the light in which
I see the queen.

LAONICE.

Oh madam, you wrong her, I take my oath, with your
baseless doubts. Put from your mind the jealous despair to
which her heart was roused by that faithless husband! If at
first she raised a bloodstained hand against her hated rival,
it was outraged pride that moved her thus savagely; after,
the vengeful anger cast about for pretexts to subside, yet
for that, there was need of time; and, to conceal no truth
from you, when I allowed myself to disobey, when for your
sake I seemed to betray her command, perhaps to her own
heart, softened by remorse, she disguised her better self and
closed her eyes to the deception, better pleased by a little
pity. Now love has set anger aside, and she looks on you
with a mother's eyes; but should I see that love forgotten,
on my oath, I shall warn you again. You know my entire
devotion to you, and besides, would the king permit any
deception?

RODOGUNE.

Whichever is crowned today, she is his mother and can
move him as she will.

LAONICE.

Whichever it is, I know he adores you; knowing how they
love, can you fear her still?

RODOGUNE.

Yes, I am afraid to wed one of them, to belong to either.

LAONICE.

Why, does neither deserve your heart?

RODOGUNE.

The same blood, the same worth claims my hand with
equal right, but it would be strange were I not more
inclined to one, despite that equality. Secret ties, sweet

Qu'un esprit combattu ne penche d'un côté.
Il est des nœuds secrets, il est des sympathies,
Dont par le doux rapport les âmes assorties
S'attachent l'une à l'autre, et se laissent piquer   360
Par ces je ne sais quoi, qu'on ne peut expliquer.
C'est par là que l'un d'eux obtient la préférence;
Je crois voir l'autre encore avec indifférence,
Mais cette indifférence est une aversion,   365
Lorsque je la compare avec ma passion.
Étrange effet d'amour! incroyable chimère!
Je voudrais être à lui, si je n'aimais son frère,
Et le plus grand des maux toutefois que je crains,
C'est que mon triste sort me livre entre ses mains.   370

LAONICE.

Ne pourrai-je servir une si belle flamme?

RODOGUNE.

Ne crois pas en tirer le secret de mon âme.
Quelque époux que le Ciel veuille me destiner,
C'est à lui pleinement que je veux me donner.
De celui que je crains si je suis le partage,   375
Je saurai l'accepter, avec même visage;
L'hymen me le rendra précieux à son tour,
Et le devoir fera ce qu'aurait fait l'amour,
Sans crainte qu'on reproche à mon humeur forcée
Qu'un autre qu'un mari règne sur ma pensée.   380

LAONICE.

Vous craignez que ma foi vous l'ose reprocher!

RODOGUNE.

Que ne puis-je à moi-même aussi bien le cacher!

LAONICE.

Quoi que vous me cachiez, aisément je devine,
Et pour vous dire enfin ce que je m'imagine,
Le Prince . . .

RODOGUNE.   Garde-toi de nommer mon vainqueur, 385
Ma rougeur trahirait les secrets de mon cœur,
Et je te voudrais mal de cette violence
Que ta dextérité ferait à mon silence.
Même de peur qu'un mot par hasard échappé
Te fasse voir ce cœur, et quels traits l'ont frappé,   390
Je romps un entretien, dont la suite me blesse.

sympathies bind two hearts together, if hearts' desires are stirred by longings that come I know not whence; but in the stirring we find our way. I am indifferent to one of them, yet compared with the love I have for his brother, that indifference is aversion! How strange are the works of love! Unbelievable dream! I would want to be his, were it not that I loved his brother! Yet the greatest mischance I fear is that my wretched fate will put me in his hands.

LAONICE.

How may I serve this marvel of love?

RODOGUNE.

Leave my secret locked away in my soul. I will belong wholly to the husband it may please Heaven to give me. If it is the one I fear, on my brow it shall seem just as if it were the other; and marriage vows will make him as precious to me, duty performing the office of love, not fearing that anyone may have the right to reproach me if someone other than a husband reigns in my soul.

LAONICE.

You cannot think that I would reproach you?

RODOGUNE.

Oh, why cannot I conceal it from myself as well?

LAONICE.

Though you may hide your heart I can easily divine, and, if I may tell you my impression, the prince—

RODOGUNE.

Take care! Do not name the victor, for blushes would unlock my heart's secret, and I should blame you, if your shrewd tongue violated my silence. And lest even a chance word might show whose heart lives in mine, I shall cut short

Adieu, mais souviens-toi que c'est sur ta promesse
Que mon esprit reprend quelque tranquillité.

LAONICE.

Madame, assurez-vous sur ma fidélité.

Fin du premier acte.

this conversation before it causes me regret. Farewell, remember my mind can be at rest again only in your promise.

LAONICE.

Be assured, madam, trust me in everything.   *Exeunt.*

End of the First Act.

ACTE II

　　　　　　　　　　　Cléopâtre.

CLÉOPÂTRE.

Serments fallacieux, salutaire contrainte,　　　　　　　395
Que m'imposa la force, et qu'accepta ma crainte,
Heureux déguisements d'un immortel courroux,
Vains fantômes d'État, évanouissez-vous.
Si d'un péril pressant la terreur vous fit naître,
Avec ce péril même il vous faut disparaître,　　　　　400
Semblables à ces vœux dans l'orage formés,
Qu'efface un prompt oubli, quand les flots sont calmés.
Et vous qu'avec tant d'art cette feinte a voilée,
Recours des impuissants, haine dissimulée,
Digne vertu des Rois, noble secret de cour,　　　　　405
Éclatez, il est temps, et voici notre jour.
Montrons-nous toutes deux, non plus comme sujettes,
Mais telle que je suis, et telle que vous êtes;
Le Parthe est éloigné, nous pouvons tout oser,
Nous n'avons rien à craindre, et rien à déguiser,　　　410
Je hais, je règne encor. Laissons d'illustres marques
En quittant, s'il le faut, ce haut rang des monarques,
Faisons-en avec gloire un départ éclatant,
Et rendons-le funeste à celle qui l'attend.
C'est encor, c'est encor cette même ennemie　　　　　415
Qui cherchait ses honneurs dedans mon infamie,
Dont la haine à son tour croit me faire la loi,
Et régner par mon ordre, et sur vous, et sur moi.
Tu m'estimes bien lâche, imprudente rivale,
Si tu crois que mon cœur jusque-là se ravale,　　　　420
Qu'il souffre qu'un hymen qu'on t'a promis en vain
Te mette ta vengeance, et mon sceptre à la main.
Vois jusqu'où m'emporta l'amour du diadème,
Vois quel sang il me coûte, et tremble pour toi-même.
Tremble, te dis-je, et songe, en dépit du traité,　　　425
Que pour t'en faire un don je l'ai trop acheté.

ACT II

[II.i]   Cleopatra *alone.*

CLEOPATRA.

False oaths, chains that kept me safe, by force my arms were bound, in my fear I gave you voice. Masks that fanned my everlasting wrath, hollow phantoms of royal craft, now be off! Harassed by danger, in terror you were born; now, with the dangers, vanish! Like vows lifted up in the raging storm, then cancelled, forgotten when the waves are calm, now begone! And you, so artfully veiled, you, shield of the impotent, you, the mask of hatred! Virtue esteemed by kings, you, noble hypocrisy of courtiers, now let shattered be your bonds! Today is ours! Now, you and I, we show who we are, servant vassals no more. The Parthian has gone; today we dare all; we have no arms to fear, none to conceal. My hatred lives, my reign endures! Let our royal step leave such prints as live in fame; if abandon we must our monarch's high state, we shall walk in a blaze of glory, and leave the throne a grave for her who waits her turn. She is the one, she is still that enemy who grasped at honor in my infamy, she who thinks her hate is now a law to me! You think me base indeed, rash rival, if you suppose my spirit sunk so low that by this marriage—it was promised in vain—I shall put scepter and vengeance in your hands. See, see how far my love of the diadem has driven me, see the blood I shed! And tremble for your own, tremble I say, and know I have bought it too dearly! Despite all treaties, it shall be no gift to you!

[II.ii]   Cléopâtre *et* Laonice.

CLÉOPÂTRE.
Laonice, vois-tu que le peuple s'apprête
Au pompeux appareil de cette grande fête?
LAONICE.
La joie en est publique, et les princes tous deux
Des Syriens ravis emportent tous les vœux.   430
L'un et l'autre fait voir un mérite si rare,
Que le souhait confus entre les deux s'égare,
Et ce qu'en quelques-uns on voit d'attachement
N'est qu'un faible ascendant d'un premier mouvement.
Ils penchent d'un côté, prêts à tomber de l'autre;   435
Leur choix pour s'affermir attend encor le vôtre,
Et de celui qu'ils font ils sont si peu jaloux,
Que votre secret su les réunira tous.
CLÉOPÂTRE.
Sais-tu que mon secret n'est pas ce que l'on pense?
LAONICE.
J'attends avec eux tous celui de leur naissance.   440
CLÉOPÂTRE.
Pour un esprit de cour, et nourri chez les grands,
Tes yeux dans leurs secrets sont bien peu pénétrants.
Apprends, ma confidente, apprends à me connaître.
Si je cache en quel rang le ciel les a fait naître,
Vois, vois que tant que l'ordre en demeure douteux,   445
Aucun des deux ne règne, et je règne pour eux.
Quoique ce soit un bien que l'un et l'autre attende,
De crainte de le perdre, aucun ne le demande.
Cependant je possède, et leur droit incertain
Me laisse avec leur sort leur sceptre dans la main: 450
Voilà mon grand secret. Sais-tu par quel mystère
Je les laissais tous deux en dépôt chez mon frère?
LAONICE.
J'ai cru qu'Antiochus les tenait éloignés,
Pour jouir des États qu'il avait regagnés.
CLÉOPÂTRE.
Il occupait leur trône et craignait leur présence,   455
Et cette juste crainte assurait ma puissance.
Mes ordres en étaient de point en point suivis,

CLEOPATRA.

Laonice, do you see how the people prepare for our great ceremonies?

LAONICE.

Joy flows in every quarter, for our two princes have captured every Syrian heart. Each displays such rare worth that the people's desire wavers, embarrassed. The attachment of some to one of them is but the slight advantage of first impressions. They lean towards one, ready to turn to the other; and to confirm their choice, they wait still for yours. Whatever their preference of the moment, they so little resent the other, that knowing your secret they will again have but one desire.

CLEOPATRA.

Did you ever think my secret may not be what the people imagine?

LAONICE.

I am as eager as any to know the story of their birth.

CLEOPATRA.

For someone who knows the court, for someone bred to life in great houses, your eyes do not pierce far into their secrets. But you shall learn, my trusted, my faithful Laonice, you shall learn what I am.

So long, you see, as the order of their birth decreed by Heaven stands in doubt, neither may rule; I reign instead; though both may expect the scepter, neither will sue for it, for fear it may escape them. Meanwhile it is mine, and their unsettled claims leave their fate, their scepter in my hands. That is my great secret! Do you know the mystery of their long stay in my brother's keeping?

LAONICE.

I thought Antiochus kept them away so that he might govern the states he had reconquered.

CLEOPATRA.

He had their throne and feared their presence; and with good reason, for through his fear I made certain of my power. My commands he obeyed, point by point, at the

Quand je le menaçais du retour de mes fils.
Voyant ce foudre prêt à suivre ma colère,
Quoi qu'il me plût oser, il n'osait me déplaire,   460
Et content malgré lui du vain titre de roi,
S'il régnait au lieu d'eux, ce n'était que sous moi.
Je te dirai bien plus. Sans violence aucune
J'aurais vu Nicanor épouser Rodogune,
Si content de lui plaire, et de me dédaigner,   465
Il eût vécu chez elle, en me laissant régner.
Son retour me fâchait plus que son hyménée,
Et j'aurais pu l'aimer, s'il ne l'eût couronnée.
Tu vis comme il y fit des efforts superflus.
Je fis beaucoup alors, et ferais encor plus,   470
S'il était quelque voie, infâme ou légitime,
Que m'enseignât la gloire, ou que m'ouvrît le crime,
Qui me pût conserver un bien que j'ai chéri
Jusqu'à verser pour lui tout le sang d'un mari.
Dans l'état pitoyable où m'en réduit la suite,   475
Délices de mon cœur, il faut que je te quitte.
On m'y force, il le faut, mais on verra quel fruit
En recevra bientôt celle qui m'y réduit.
L'amour que j'ai pour toi tourne en haine pour elle :
Autant que l'un fut grand, l'autre sera cruelle,   480
Et puisqu'en te perdant, j'ai sur qui m'en venger,
Ma perte est supportable, et mon mal est léger.

LAONICE.

Quoi ! vous parlez encor de vengeance et de haine
Pour celle dont vous-même allez faire une reine !

CLÉOPÂTRE.

Quoi ! je ferais un Roi pour être son époux,   485
Et m'exposer aux traits de son juste courroux !
N'apprendras-tu jamais, âme basse et grossière,
A voir par d'autres yeux que les yeux du vulgaire ?
Toi qui connais ce peuple, et sais qu'aux champs de Mars
Lâchement d'une femme il suit les étendards,   490
Que sans Antiochus Tryphon m'eût dépouillée,
Que sous lui son ardeur fut soudain réveillée,
Ne saurais-tu juger que si je nomme un roi,
C'est pour le commander, et combattre pour moi ?
J'en ai le choix en main avec le droit d'aînesse,   495

mere threat of their return. Seeing the thunderbolt I had
to enforce my will, there was no limit to my daring, and he
dared not risk my displeasure. He must content himself
with the empty name and mantle of king, for if he reigned
in place of my sons, it was under me. I will tell you still
more: Nicanor might have wed his Rodogune without fear
of my revenge, had he but remained content to please her
and despise me, had he but lived in her land, leaving me to
reign over mine. His return to Syria, that enraged me more
than their marriage: I could have loved her, had he not
wished to crown her queen. You saw his useless efforts. I
did much then, and I would do still more, to find some
path, hellish or lawful, lit by glory or opened by crime,
whereby I could keep a crown I loved so much that it cost
my husband his blood. And now in this wretched hour,
heart of my heart [*holding the crown*], I must leave you. They
force me, I must; but they will see what good comes to her
who brings me to this. My love for you is hate for her! As
great the one, cruel the other! But since I have a victim to
pay for my loss, I can bear it; I can slight the pain.

LAONICE.

Oh! You talk of vengeance still, you hate her, whom you
yourself have chosen as queen?

CLEOPATRA.

Oh! I should crown a king to give her a husband, and
leave myself without defense before her natural anger?
Will you never learn, you coarse, mean-spirited creature,
to see but with the eyes of the vulgar crowd! You know my
people, you know that under a woman's banner they are
cowards on the field of Mars. But for Antiochus, Tryphon
would have stripped me bare; under Antiochus at once
their spirits revived. You might see at least that when I
crown a king, it is to rule over him; I do so that he may fight
my wars. The choice lies with me, with the right of prior

Et puisqu'il en faut faire une aide à ma faiblesse,
Que la guerre sans lui ne peut se rallumer,
J'userai bien du droit que j'ai de le nommer.
On ne montera point au rang dont je dévale,
Qu'en épousant ma haine au lieu de ma rivale: 500
Ce n'est qu'en me vengeant qu'on me le peut ravir,
Et je ferai régner qui me voudra servir.

LAONICE.

Je vous connaissais mal.

CLÉOPÂTRE.   Connais-moi tout entière.
Quand je mis Rodogune en tes mains prisonnière,
Ce ne fut ni pitié ni respect de son rang   505
Qui m'arrêta le bras et conserva son sang.
La mort d'Antiochus me laissait sans armée,
Et d'une troupe en hâte à me suivre animée,
Beaucoup dans ma vengeance ayant fini leurs jours,
M'exposaient à son frère et faible et sans secours.   510
Je me voyais perdue, à moins d'un tel otage.
Il vint, et sa fureur craignit pour ce cher gage;
Il m'imposa des lois, exigea des serments,
Et moi, j'accordai tout, pour obtenir du temps.
Le temps est un trésor plus grand qu'on ne peut croire: 515
J'en obtins, et je crus obtenir la victoire.
J'ai pu reprendre haleine, et sous de faux apprêts . . .
Mais voici mes deux fils, que j'ai mandés exprès:
Écoute, et tu verras quel est cet hyménée
Où se doit terminer cette illustre journée.   520

[II.iii]   Cléopâtre, Antiochus, Séleucus, Laonice.

CLÉOPÂTRE.

Mes enfants, prenez place. Enfin voici le jour
Si doux à mes souhaits, si cher à mon amour,
Où je puis voir briller sur une de vos têtes
Ce que j'ai conservé parmi tant de tempêtes,
Et vous remettre un bien, après tant de malheurs,   525
Qui m'a coûté pour vous tant de soins et de pleurs.
Il peut vous souvenir quelles furent mes larmes,
Quand Tryphon me donna de si rudes alarmes,
Que pour ne vous pas voir exposés à ses coups,

birth, and since my weakness must be helped, since without that help no war can be resumed, I shall use well my
right to choose the king. No one rises to the rank I resign
unless he espouses my hatred, rather than my rival! The
crown can be taken from me only by taking up my vengeance; I will set on the throne no man but my willing
servant!

LAONICE.

I did not know you!

CLEOPATRA.

Know me through and through! When I put Rodogune
under your guard, I checked my wrath, I spared her life
not from respect of rank, not from pity. When Antiochus
died I lost my army; and of the few troops hastily pressed
into service, many had perished for the sake of my vengeance. I was exposed, feeble, helpless before her brother's
advance. I knew I was lost without such a hostage. He came
raging, but in fear for the hostage so cherished. He imposed conditions; he demanded oaths of treaty, and I
granted them, anything to gain time. For time is the
treasure, greater than a man can think! And time I gained,
and thought I held the palm of victory. Then could I catch
my breath and with counterfeit preparations, with these—
But wait, here are my two sons that I sent for just now.
Listen and see the kind of wedding I have planned to end
this day of days.

[II.iii]   *Enter* Antiochus *and* Seleucus.

CLEOPATRA.

Children, come sit near me. At last, here is the day, the
hoped for, the longed for day that may ease my loving
heart; the day I shall see on one of your brows the shining
crown I preserved through so many storms, when I restore
to you after so much grief the birthright that has cost such
trouble, such tears. You remember perhaps the tears I shed,
when Tryphon alarmed us so grievously, when to save you
from his attack I resolved to lose you to myself. What grief

Il fallut me résoudre à me priver de vous. 530
Quelles peines depuis, grands Dieux, n'ai-je souffertes!
Chaque jour redoubla mes douleurs et mes pertes.
Je vis votre royaume entre ces murs réduit,
Je crus mort votre père, et sur un si faux bruit
Le peuple mutiné voulut avoir un maître. 535
J'eus beau le nommer lâche, ingrat, parjure, traître,
Il fallut satisfaire à son brutal désir,
Et de peur qu'il en prît, il m'en fallut choisir.
Pour vous sauver l'État que n'eussé-je pu faire?
Je choisis un époux avec des yeux de mère, 540
Votre oncle Antiochus, et j'espérai qu'en lui
Votre trône tombant trouverait un appui.
Mais à peine son bras en relève la chute,
Que par lui de nouveau le sort me persécute.
Maître de votre État par sa valeur sauvé, 545
Il s'obstine à remplir ce trône relevé.
Qui lui parle de vous attire sa menace,
Il n'a défait Tryphon que pour prendre sa place,
Et de dépositaire et de libérateur,
Il s'érige en tyran et lâche usurpateur. 550
Sa main l'en a puni, pardonnons à son ombre.
Aussi bien en un seul voici des maux sans nombre.
   Nicanor votre père et mon premier époux . . .
Mais pourquoi lui donner encor des noms si doux,
Puisque l'ayant cru mort, il sembla ne revivre 555
Que pour s'en dépouiller afin de nous poursuivre?
Passons, je ne me puis souvenir, sans trembler,
Du coup dont j'empêchai qu'il nous pût accabler.
Je ne sais s'il est digne ou d'horreur ou d'estime,
S'il plut aux Dieux ou non, s'il fut justice ou crime, 560
Mais soit crime ou justice, il est certain, mes fils,
Que mon amour pour vous fit tout ce que je fis.
Ni celui des grandeurs, ni celui de la vie
Ne jeta dans mon cœur cette aveugle furie.
J'étais lasse d'un trône où d'éternels malheurs 565
Me comblaient chaque jour de nouvelles douleurs.
Ma vie est presque usée, et ce reste inutile
Chez mon frère avec vous trouvait un sûr asile.
Mais voir après douze ans et de soins et de maux

have I not suffered since then, Gods above! Each day
doubled my loss and my sorrows: your kingdom shrunk
within the walls of this city, your father dead, as I thought;
and on that false rumor, the mutinous people demanded a
master. Coward, ingrate, faithless, traitor—they bore every
insult if only I would satisfy their brutish will. In certain
fear they would have a king, I determined at least to make
the choice myself. To preserve your state, is there anything
I would not have done? It was a mother's eyes that chose
my husband, your uncle Antiochus, in the hope he might
shore up your tottering throne. But no sooner had his
sword stayed its fall than the Fates made of him a new
threat. The strong arm that had saved this realm stub-
bornly held your throne for himself. A mention of you
brought upon the one who spoke his wrath, and Tryphon
he had conquered only to take his place: from your
guardian, your liberator sprang a tyrant, a vile usurper.
He has been punished, by his own hand; therefore let his
memory be pardoned. And from only one came evils un-
numbered.

Nicanor, your father, my first husband—but why accord
him those titles when, thinking he was dead, I saw him
return to life only to cast them off himself, the better to
work our downfall? But no more of that, I cannot recall
without shudders the disaster that but for me he would have
inflicted on us. And whether it deserves horror or praise,
whether it pleased the gods or not, whether it was justice or
crime, I do not know; but this is certain, my sons, my love
for you was the root of all I did. No thirst for glory, no love
of life could have ignited that blind fury in my heart. I
tired of a throne beset from day to endless day with pain
and misfortune. My life was worn out, and safe in my
brother's realm with you I might have spent those remain-
ing useless hours. But to see a father wrest from you the
reward of twelve years' painful effort! But to see your crown

Un père vous ôter le fruit de mes travaux!   570
Mais voir votre couronne après lui destinée
Aux enfants qui naîtraient d'un second hyménée!
A cette indignité je ne connus plus rien,
Je me crus tout permis pour garder votre bien.
Recevez donc, mes fils, de la main d'une mère   575
Un trône racheté par le malheur d'un père.
Je crus qu'il fit lui-même un crime en vous l'ôtant,
Et si j'en ai fait un en vous le rachetant,
Daigne du juste ciel la bonté souveraine,
Vous en laissant le fruit, m'en réserver la peine,   580
Ne lancer que sur moi les foudres mérités,
Et n'épandre sur vous que des prospérités!

ANTIOCHUS.

Jusques ici, Madame, aucun ne met en doute
Les longs et grands travaux que notre amour vous coûte,
Et nous croyons tenir des soins de cette amour   585
Ce doux espoir du trône aussi bien que le jour.
Le récit nous en charme, et nous fait mieux comprendre
Quelles grâces tous deux nous vous en devons rendre.
Mais afin qu'à jamais nous les puissions bénir,
Épargnez le dernier à notre souvenir.   590
Ce sont fatalités dont l'âme embarrassée
A plus qu'elle ne veut se voit souvent forcée.
Sur les noires couleurs d'un si triste tableau
Il faut passer l'éponge, ou tirer le rideau.
Un fils est criminel, quand il les examine,   595
Et quelque suite enfin que le ciel y destine,
J'en rejette l'idée, et crois qu'en ces malheurs,
Le silence ou l'oubli nous sied mieux que les pleurs.
Nous attendons le sceptre avec même espérance,
Mais si nous l'attendons, c'est sans impatience.   600
Nous pouvons sans régner vivre tous deux contents.
C'est le fruit de vos soins, jouissez-en longtemps.
Il tombera sur nous quand vous en serez lasse,
Nous le recevrons lors de bien meilleure grâce,
Et l'accepter sitôt semble nous reprocher   605
De n'être revenus que pour vous l'arracher.

SÉLEUCUS

J'ajouterai, Madame, à ce qu'a dit mon frère,

pass from him to children of another's bed! The shame
drove me out of myself: to save what belonged to you I
recognized no law! This throne, then, regained with your
father's ill fortune, take it, it is from your mother's hand.
Could I doubt that his was the crime, to steal it from you?
And if restoring it to you is mine, may Heaven's justice do
kind sanction and punish me, leaving you the gain: may
its thunder strike my head, so all its blessings rain down on
yours.

ANTIOCHUS.

No one doubts, madam, that the labors of love you performed for us have been long and great; and we know well
we owe all hope of kingship to your love and care, as well
as our lives. The story moves us deeply; we comprehend
better still the infinite gratitude that must be our payment.
But so that we might forever gratefully receive these
blessings, help us blot the last from memory: the Fates too
often force unwilling souls to mortal deeds. The darker
colors must be washed away, the curtains drawn before a
picture so tragic. It would be criminal in sons to linger
there. Let Heaven set what sanction it will, I put aside even
the thought, and think that in these misfortunes, silence
and oblivion are more fitting than tears. We await the
scepter with equal hope, but we wait without impatience.
We live content without the pleasures of rule. They are
your reward; for your past cares, enjoy them long years
more. Let them come to us when they are a burden to you.
It will appear then more gracious in us to accept them,
rather than on this day, when it might seem we are here
only to steal them from you.

SELEUCUS.

There is left for me but this, madam, to add to my

Que bien qu'avec plaisir et l'un et l'autre espère,
L'ambition n'est pas notre plus grand désir.
Régnez, nous le verrons tous deux avec plaisir,   610
Et c'est bien la raison que pour tant de puissance
Nous vous rendions du moins un peu d'obéissance,
Et que celui de nous dont le ciel a fait choix
Sous votre illustre exemple apprenne l'art des rois.

CLÉOPÂTRE.

Dites tout, mes enfants. Vous fuyez la couronne,   615
Non que son trop d'éclat ou son poids vous étonne:
L'unique fondement de cette aversion,
C'est la honte attachée à sa possession.
Elle passe à vos yeux pour la même infamie,
S'il faut la partager avec notre ennemie,   620
Et qu'un indigne hymen la fasse retomber
Sur celle qui venait pour vous la dérober.
  O nobles sentiments d'une âme généreuse!
O fils vraiment mes fils! ô mère trop heureuse!
Le sort de votre père enfin est éclairci,   625
Il était innocent, et je puis l'être aussi;
Il vous aima toujours, et ne fut mauvais père
Que charmé par la sœur, ou forcé par le frère,
Et dans cette embuscade où son effort fut vain,
Rodogune, mes fils, le tua par ma main.   630
Ainsi de cet amour la fatale puissance
Vous coûte votre père, à moi mon innocence,
Et si ma main pour vous n'avait tout attenté,
L'effet de cet amour vous aurait tout coûté.
Ainsi vous me rendrez l'innocence et l'estime,   635
Lorsque vous punirez la cause de mon crime.
De cette même main qui vous a tout sauvé,
Dans son sang odieux je l'aurais bien lavé,
Mais comme vous aviez votre part aux offenses,
Je vous ai réservé votre part aux vengeances,   640
Et pour ne tenir plus en suspens vos esprits,
Si vous voulez régner, le trône est à ce prix.
Entre deux fils que j'aime avec même tendresse,
Embrasser ma querelle est le seul droit d'aînesse:
La mort de Rodogune en nommera l'aîné.   645
  Quoi! vous montrez tous deux un visage étonné!

brother's words. Ambition spurs both, yet for us another desire is stronger. Continue in your reign; we obey you with pleasure, for it is only just that in return for those great powers we offer our duty, and that the one Heaven has chosen may learn the royal arts of rule by your illustrious example.

CLEOPATRA.

Why will you not say it all, my children? Say you shun the crown, not because it weighs too heavily, shines too bright! Say the single cause of your aversion is shame, the shame attached to its possession. Say that in your eyes it would be the deepest infamy to share it with your enemy, that by a shameful marriage it will fall to the woman who had come to steal it from you.

Feelings of that nobility live in great hearts only! Ah, my sons, sons truly mine! Could there be a mother more fortunate! At last the veil of your father's destiny is rent! He was guiltless, I may be innocent too! He loved you still, and if the father was false to his children, it was an evil spell cast by that sister, he was compelled by that brother; and in that ambush, where all his purpose was rendered vain, it was Rodogune, my sons, who slew him by my hand! That fatal passion's power cost you your father, me my innocence. For had not my hand dared all, the end of that passion would have cost you all. You win back my innocence, my good name, when you punish the cause of my crime. The very hand that saved all you have I might now wash in that detested blood; but as you have a share in the injury, I have saved you your share in our vengeance! To keep you in suspense no longer: if you would reign, ascend the throne at this price. Of two sons I love with equal tenderness, the elder is he who makes my quarrel his own. The death of Rodogune will announce his birth!

Well! What! Astonishment in both your faces? Do you

44 *Rodogune* [II.iv

Redoutez-vous son frère? Après la paix infâme,
Que même en la jurant je détestais dans l'âme,
J'ai fait lever des gens par des ordres secrets,
Qu'à vous suivre en tous lieux vous trouverez tous prêts; 650
Et tandis qu'il fait tête aux princes d'Arménie,
Nous pouvons sans péril briser sa tyrannie.
Qui vous fait donc pâlir à cette juste loi?
Est-ce pitié pour elle? Est-ce haine pour moi?
Voulez-vous l'épouser, afin qu'elle me brave, 655
Et mettre mon destin aux mains de mon esclave?
Vous ne répondez point! Allez, enfants ingrats,
Pour qui je crus en vain conserver ces États,
J'ai fait votre oncle roi, j'en ferai bien un autre,
Et mon nom peut encore ici plus que le vôtre. 660

SÉLEUCUS.

Mais, Madame, voyez que pour premier exploit...

CLÉOPÂTRE.

Mais que chacun de vous pense à ce qu'il me doit.
Je sais bien que le sang qu'à vos mains je demande
N'est pas le digne essai d'une valeur bien grande,
Mais si vous me devez et le sceptre et le jour, 665
Ce doit être envers moi le sceau de votre amour.
Sans ce gage ma haine à jamais s'en défie;
Ce n'est qu'en m'imitant que l'on me justifie.
    Rien ne vous sert ici de faire les surpris,
Je vous le dis encor, le trône est à ce prix. 670
Je puis en disposer comme de ma conquête.
Point d'aîné, point de roi, qu'en m'apportant sa tête,
Et puisque mon seul choix vous y peut élever,
Pour jouir de mon crime, il le faut achever.

[II.iv]   Séleucus *et* Antiochus.

SÉLEUCUS.

Est-il une constance à l'épreuve du foudre 675
    Dont ce cruel arrêt met notre espoir en poudre?

ANTIOCHUS.

Est-il un coup de foudre à comparer aux coups
    Que ce cruel arrêt vient de lancer sur nous?

fear her brother? Since that infamous truce, that I
abominated as my tongue swore to it, I have levied troops
in secret, ready to follow you anywhere, and while he
drives back the princes of Armenia we may safely break his
tyranny here. What, you blench at my just command? Do
you pity her? Is it me you hate? Will you marry her, knowing she will defy me, knowing you have given my slave
power over my life? No answer! Ungrateful, unnatural
children! For this I preserved your kingdom! Your uncle
was king by my command, another may be again, for my
voice is stronger here than yours.

SELEUCUS.

But, madam, you must see that as our first royal command—

CLEOPATRA.

But you and you, sirs, must remember what is due to me! I
see well enough that the blood I expect at your hands is but
a poor test of your great valor. But as you owe me your
lives, your scepter, let that blood be the seal of your love.
Without that pledge, my hate must forever suspect your
faith. You can justify me only if you follow my example.

It is no use to pretend surprise. I tell you again, that is
the cost of your throne. It is mine by conquest; I give it
where I will. There will be no first-born, no king, who does
not come to me with her head. Only my word can raise you
to the throne; before you taste the fruits of my crime,
finish it yourselves!   [*Exeunt* Cleopatra *and* Laonice.]

[II.iv]

SELEUCUS.

Can we live, shattered by the cruelty of that command?

ANTIOCHUS.

Can Heaven threaten a more shattering bolt than this
cruel command?

SÉLEUCUS.

O haines, ô fureurs dignes d'une Mégère!
O femme, que je n'ose appeler encor mère!   680
Après que tes fortaits ont régné pleinement,
Ne saurais-tu souffrir qu'on règne innocemment?
Quels attraits penses-tu qu'ait pour nous la couronne,
S'il faut qu'un crime égal par ta main nous la donne,
Et de quelles horreurs nous doit-elle combler,   685
Si pour monter au trône il faut te ressembler?

ANTIOCHUS.

Gardons plus de respect aux droits de la nature,
Et n'imputons qu'au sort notre triste aventure:
Nous le nommions cruel, mais il nous était doux,
Quand il ne nous donnait à combattre que nous.   690
Confidents tout ensemble et rivaux l'un de l'autre,
Nous ne concevions point de mal pareil au nôtre.
Cependant à nous voir l'un de l'autre rivaux,
Nous ne concevions pas la moitié de nos maux.

SÉLEUCUS.

Une douleur si sage et si respectueuse   695
Ou n'est guère sensible ou guère impétueuse,
Et c'est en de tels maux avoir l'esprit bien fort,
D'en connaître la cause, et l'imputer au sort.
Pour moi, je sens les miens avec plus de faiblesse:
Plus leur cause m'est chère, et plus l'effet m'en blesse.   700
Non que pour m'en venger j'ose entreprendre rien,
Je donnerais encor tout mon sang pour le sien.
Je sais ce que je dois; mais dans cette contrainte,
Si je retiens mon bras, je laisse aller ma plainte,
Et j'estime qu'au point qu'elle nous a blessés,   705
Qui ne fait que s'en plaindre a du respect assez.
Voyez-vous bien quel est le ministère infâme
Qu'ose exiger de nous la haine d'une femme?
Voyez-vous qu'aspirant à des crimes nouveaux,
De deux princes ses fils elle fait ses bourreaux?   710
Si vous pouvez le voir, pouvez-vous vous en taire?

ANTIOCHUS.

Je vois bien plus encor, je vois qu'elle est ma mère,
Et plus je vois son crime indigne de ce rang,
Plus je lui vois souiller la source de mon sang.

SELEUCUS.

Ah, hatred, fury! Fury of the Furies! Ah, woman! I dare
not call you Mother still! Your crimes have reigned long
enough, can you not suffer us to reign with innocence? Do
you think we are so drawn to a crown that we would take it
with crimes like yours? What horrors are not heaped on
our heads if we ascend the throne by your evil path?

ANTIOCHUS.

We should speak with more respect of a natural tie, and
heap on fate alone the guilt of our wretchedness. It was
cruel, we said, but how kind, when we had only ourselves
to combat. In mutual trust but at the same time rivals,
neither could imagine a misfortune equal to ours; per-
plexed in that rivalry we did not see half the evils to come.

SELEUCUS.

Your restrained sorrow, your smooth respect! How little
that shows of feeling and spirit! In such an evil pass, it is
strong-minded indeed to know the cause and impute responsibility only to Fate. As for me, the torture gains on my
weaker strength. The more dear to me the source, the
deeper my wound. Not that I dare think of revenge; for I
know what I owe, and I would venture my blood for hers.
But if I restrain my hand, I may loose my complaint. In my
eyes, she has so wounded us that only to complain is
respect enough. Do you not see the infamous work this
woman's hate dares exact from us? Do you not see,
breathing new crimes, she would put the executioner's ax
in the hands of princes, and her sons! That you can see and
hold your tongue?

ANTIOCHUS.

I see that and much more: I see she is my mother, and the
better I see her crime dishonors the name, the more clearly
I see it stains the very springs of my blood. The violence of

J'en sens de ma douleur croître la violence,   715
Mais ma confusion m'impose le silence,
Lorsque dans ses forfaits sur nos fronts imprimés
Je vois les traits honteux dont nous sommes formés.
Je tâche à cet objet d'être aveugle ou stupide,
J'ose me déguiser jusqu'à son parricide,   720
Je me cache à moi-même un excès de malheur
Où notre ignominie égale ma douleur,
Et détournant les yeux d'une mère cruelle,
J'impute tout au sort, qui m'a fait naître d'elle.
      Je conserve pourtant encore un peu d'espoir :   725
Elle est mère, et le sang a beaucoup de pouvoir.
Et le sort l'eût-il faite encor plus inhumaine,
Une larme d'un fils peut amollir sa haine.

SÉLEUCUS.

Ah ! mon frère, l'amour n'est guère véhément
Pour des fils élevés dans un bannissement,   730
Et qu'ayant fait nourrir presque dans l'esclavage
Elle n'a rappelés que pour servir sa rage.
De ses pleurs tant vantés je découvre le fard,
Nous avons en son cœur, vous et moi, peu de part ;
Elle fait bien sonner ce grand amour de mère,   735
Mais elle seule enfin s'aime, et se considère,
Et quoi que nous étale un langage si doux,
Elle a tout fait pour elle, et n'a rien fait pour nous.
Ce n'est qu'un faux amour que la haine domine,
Nous ayant embrassés, elle nous assassine,   740
En veut au cher objet dont nous sommes épris,
Nous demande son sang, met le trône à ce prix !
Ce n'est plus de sa main qu'il nous le faut attendre.
Il est, il est à nous, si nous osons le prendre.
Notre révolte ici n'a rien que d'innocent,   745
Il est à l'un de nous, si l'autre le consent.
Régnons, et son courroux ne sera que faiblesse,
C'est l'unique moyen de sauver la Princesse.
Allons la voir, mon frère, et demeurons unis :
C'est l'unique moyen de voir nos maux finis.   750
Je forme un beau dessein que son amour m'inspire,
Mais il faut qu'avec lui notre union conspire.
Notre amour aujourd'hui si digne de pitié
Ne saurait triompher que par notre amitié.

my sorrow increases, but in confusion I am silenced. Better be stupid, better be blind, than see in those features, those that are impressed on our own, the shameful mark of her transgressions printed on our brow. I dare even cover the parricide, I hide from my own eyes the unbearable disgrace, knowing our ignominy is no less than our pain. Turning away from this mother's cruelty, I blame all on the fate that I was born to her.

But there is yet one slight hope. She is a mother, and blood is strong. Had the fates made her more inhuman still, the tears of a son may yet soften her wrath.

SELEUCUS.

Ah, Antiochus, the love for sons reared in exile is often moderate. We were bred almost in servitude, and she has called us home merely to serve her rage. She may boast of streaming tears; I see the painted eye beneath, and in her heart you and I have little place. A great mother-love rings loud in her mouth, but in the end it is herself, only herself that she loves and serves. In soft accents she spreads before our eyes a gentle prospect, but it is for herself, not for me nor for you. There is only counterfeit love, mastered by hate. In her embrace, she murders us. In anger toward the woman who has our hearts, she demands blood at our hands; she sets thus the ransom of a throne. We should no longer expect it from her hand: it is ours, if we dare take it. We rebel in perfect innocence: it is yours or mine, if the other consents. Let us take the scepter, and her wrath is helpless. That is the only way to save the princess. We must find her and remain united. That is the only way to see an end to these evils. A splendid plan takes form, inspired by love for her; but we must conspire together, as one mind, one spirit. Our passion today so pitiable can gain its cause only through our love one for the other.

ANTIOCHUS.

Cet avertissement marque une défiance   755
Que la mienne pour vous souffre avec patience.
Allons, et soyez sûr que même le trépas
Ne peut rompre des nœuds que l'amour ne rompt pas.

Fin du deuxième acte.

ANTIOCHUS.

>The warning hints a doubt that, in my love for you, I must suffer patiently. Come, you may be sure death itself will drive no wedge where love cannot make a breach.

[*Exeunt.*]

End of the Second Act.

ACTE III

RODOGUNE.

Voilà comme l'amour succède à la colère,
Comme elle ne me voit qu'avec des yeux de mère,   760
Comme elle aime la paix, comme elle fait un roi,
Et comme elle use enfin de ses fils, et de moi.
Et tantôt mes soupçons lui faisaient une offense?
Elle n'avait rien fait qu'en sa juste défense?
Lorsque tu la trompais elle fermait les yeux?   765
Ah! que ma défiance en jugeait beaucoup mieux!
Tu le vois, Laonice.

LAONICE.   Et vous voyez, Madame,
Quelle fidélité vous conserve mon âme,
Et qu'ayant reconnu sa haine et mon erreur,
Le cœur gros de soupirs, et frémissant d'horreur,   770
Je romps une foi due aux secrets de ma reine,
Et vous viens découvrir mon erreur et sa haine.

RODOGUNE.

Cet avis salutaire est l'unique secours
A qui je crois devoir le reste de mes jours.
Mais ce n'est pas assez de m'avoir avertie,   775
Il faut de ces périls m'aplanir la sortie,
Il faut que tes conseils m'aident à repousser . . .

LAONICE.

Madame, au nom des Dieux, veuillez m'en dispenser;
C'est assez que pour vous je lui sois infidèle,
Sans m'engager encore à des conseils contre elle.   780
Oronte est avec vous, qui, comme ambassadeur,
Devait de cet hymen honorer la splendeur;
Comme c'est en ses mains que le Roi votre frère
A déposé le soin d'une tête si chère,
Je vous laisse avec lui pour en délibérer;   785
Quoi que vous résolviez, laissez-moi l'ignorer.
Au reste, assurez-vous de l'amour des deux princes.
Plutôt que de vous perdre, ils perdront leurs provinces,

ACT III

[III.i]   Rodogune, Orontes, Laonice.

RODOGUNE.

And so that is how love follows on hate, how she looks on
me with a mother's eye? That is how she loves peace and
how she will crown the king, how she will treat her sons
and me! A moment ago my suspicions were unjust! All she
has done was in her own just defense, and she averted her
eyes from your deceptions! Ah, my suspicious mind was
the better judge. You see that now, Laonice?

LAONICE.

And you see, madam, that in spirit I keep faith with you.
My heart swelled with pity, shuddered with horror when I
recognized her hate and my misjudgment, and now I break
faith coming to you with my error and her secret hate.

RODOGUNE.

You will have saved my life; what remains to me I owe
entirely to this warning. But to give the alarm is not
enough; you must smooth my way out of this danger. You
must advise me how to ward off—

LAONICE.

In the Gods' name, madam, relieve me of that duty, I beg
you; I betray a trust, that must be enough. I cannot conspire against her, advising you. You have Orontes, who as
ambassador was to add luster to your wedding day; and as
your brother entrusted your safety to him, I leave you with
him to take counsel. Whatever you may decide, let me not
know of it. I can say only this, make certain of the love of
the two princes. They would rather lose a kingdom than

Mais je ne réponds pas que ce cœur inhumain
Ne veuille à leur refus s'armer d'une autre main.   790
Je vous parle en tremblant : si j'étais ici vue,
Votre péril croîtrait, et je serais perdue.
Fuyez, grande princesse, et souffrez cet adieu.

RODOGUNE.

Va, je reconnaîtrai ce service en son lieu.

[III.ii]   Rodogune *et* Oronte.

RODOGUNE.

Que ferons-nous, Oronte, en ce péril extrême,   795
Où l'on fait de mon sang le prix d'un diadème ?
Fuirons-nous chez mon frère ? attendrons-nous la mort ?
Ou ferons-nous contre elle un généreux effort ?

ORONTE.

Notre fuite, Madame, est assez difficile :
J'ai vu des gens de guerre épandus par la ville.   800
Si l'on veut votre perte, on vous fait observer ;
Ou s'il vous est permis encor de vous sauver,
L'avis de Laonice est sans doute une adresse :
Feignant de vous servir elle sert sa maîtresse.
La Reine, qui surtout craint de vous voir régner,   805
Vous donne ces terreurs pour vous faire éloigner,
Et pour rompre un hymen qu'avec peine elle endure,
Elle en veut à vous-même imputer la rupture.
Elle obtiendra par vous le but de ses souhaits,
Et vous accusera de violer la paix ;   810
Et le Roi, plus piqué contre vous que contre elle,
Vous voyant lui porter une guerre nouvelle,
Blâmera vos frayeurs et nos légèretés,
D'avoir osé douter de la foi des traités,
Et peut-être, pressé des guerres d'Arménie,   815
Vous laissera moquée, et la Reine impunie.
    A ces honteux moyens gardez de recourir :
C'est ici qu'il vous faut ou régner ou périr.
Le ciel pour vous ailleurs n'a point fait de couronne,
Et l'on s'en rend indigne alors qu'on l'abandonne.   820

RODOGUNE.

Ah ! que de vos conseils j'aimerais la vigueur,

you. However, I can give no assurance that her flinty heart
will not arm others against you, if they reject her command. I tremble even in speaking to you; should I be seen
here, your perils would increase and I should be lost. You
must flee, great princess, and, pardon me, farewell.

RODOGUNE.

Yes, go, I shall repay your service, when it is possible.

Exit Laonice.

[III.ii]

RODOGUNE.

What can be done, Orontes, in this extreme danger, when
the crown is offered as a prize for my blood? Shall we flee
and go to join my brother? Or must we wait for death here?
Can we summon the courage to resist?

ORONTES.

Escape would be more than difficult, madam. I have seen
armed guards everywhere in the city. If the order is to destroy you, you will be watched, or if it is to let you escape,
Laonice's warning is almost certainly a trap; pretending to
help you, she obeys her mistress. The queen fears most of all
to see you on the throne, and intends to frighten you away.
A wedding she cannot endure she will have stopped, but so
as to throw the responsibility on you. Through you she will
reach her goals, and accuse you of violating the treaty. For
then the king, more aroused against you than against her,
since it is you who brings a new war upon him, will accuse
you of faint-heartedness, of too lightly disregarding an
oath of treaty, and perhaps, hard-pressed as he is by the
Armenians, he will leave you here an object of scorn, and
the queen will go unpunished.

Do not venture on that ignoble path: here you must reign
or perish! Other than here, Heaven has chosen no diadem
for you. To surrender it would be contemptible.

RODOGUNE.

How welcome such bracing advice would be, if the strength

Si nous avions la force égale à ce grand coeur!
Mais pourrons-nous braver une Reine en colère
Avec ce peu de gens que m'a laissés mon frère?

ORONTE.

J'aurais perdu l'esprit, si j'osais me vanter   825
Qu'avec ce peu de gens nous pussions résister.
Nous mourrons à vos pieds, c'est toute l'assistance
Que vous peut en ces lieux offrir notre impuissance.
Mais pouvez-vous trembler, quand dans ces mêmes lieux
Vous portez le grand maître et des rois et des Dieux?   830
L'amour fera lui seul tout ce qu'il vous faut faire.
Faites-vous un rempart des fils contre la mère,
Ménagez bien leur flamme, ils voudront tout pour vous,
Et ces astres naissants sont adorés de tous.
Quoi que puisse en ces lieux une reine cruelle,   835
Pouvant tout sur ses fils, vous y pouvez plus qu'elle.
Cependant trouvez bon qu'en ces extrémités
Je tâche à rassembler nos Parthes écartés.
Ils sont peu, mais vaillants, et peuvent de sa rage
Empêcher la surprise et le premier outrage.   840
Craignez moins, et surtout, Madame, en ce grand jour,
Si vous voulez régner, faites régner l'amour.

[III.iii]   Rodogune.

RODOGUNE.

Quoi? je pourrais descendre à ce lâche artifice
D'aller de mes amants mendier le service,
Et sous l'indigne appas d'un coup d'œil affété,   845
J'irais jusqu'en leur cœur chercher ma sûreté?
Celles de ma naissance ont horreur des bassesses,
Leur sang tout généreux hait ces molles adresses.
Quel que soit le secours qu'ils me puissent offrir,
Je croirai faire assez de le daigner souffrir.   850
Je verrai leur amour, j'éprouverai sa force,
Sans flatter leurs désirs, sans leur jeter d'amorce,
Et s'il est assez fort pour me servir d'appui,
Je le ferai régner, mais en régnant sur lui.
    Sentiments étouffés de colère et de haine,   855
Rallumez vos flambeaux à celles de la Reine,

of our arms were equal to our courage! But how can we
defy the queen's anger with the mere handful of men my
brother left me?

ORONTES.

I would be mad to boast that we can resist with so few
men. We shall die at your feet; that is all the help our
powerless arms can give you here. But why do you
tremble, when in this very place you have by your side the
king of kings, the god of the Gods? The god of love himself
will be your guard. Make of the sons a rampart against the
mother! Encourage them, flatter their desires; for your sake
they will do anything. These new stars in our sky are wor-
shipped by all the Syrians. Whatever command the cruel
queen may give, while her sons can deny you nothing, you
are stronger than she. In the meantime, if in this great
peril you approve, I will call together our scattered
Parthians. They are few indeed, but valiant; they can
prevent a surprise attack or an unexpected outrage. Be
strong, madam, and if you would reign tomorrow, let Love
reign today.   *Exit* Orontes.

[III.iii]

RODOGUNE.

Oh, could I sink so low as to beg and sue for my lovers'
aid, and shamefully, with false seductive eyes, look for
safety in their very hearts? Women of birth abhor these
abject tricks; their noble blood recoils from all effeminate
cunning. Whatever support they propose themselves, I can
deign only to receive their offer. I will see this love, test its
strength; but no flattering encouragement, no promises; if
it is strong for my defense, I shall let love rule, but it shall
be ruled by me.

Smothered passions of anger and hate, your torches burn
here again; take fire at the fires of the queen and melt these

Et d'un oubli contraint rompez la dure loi,
Pour rendre enfin justice aux mânes d'un grand roi.
Rapportez à mes yeux son image sanglante,
D'amour et de fureur encore étincelante,   860
Telle que je le vis, quand tout percé de coups
Il me cria : «Vengeance! Adieu, je meurs pour vous!»
Chère ombre, hélas! bien loin de l'avoir poursuivie,
J'allais baiser la main qui t'arracha la vie,
Rendre un respect de fille à qui versa ton sang;   865
Mais pardonne au devoir que m'impose mon rang.
Plus la haute naissance approche des couronnes,
Plus cette grandeur même asservit nos personnes.
Nous n'avons point de cœur pour aimer ni haïr :
Toutes nos passions ne savent qu'obéir.   870
Après avoir armé pour venger cet outrage,
D'une paix mal conçue on m'a faite le gage,
Et moi, fermant les yeux sur ce noir attentat,
Je suivais mon destin en victime d'État.
Mais aujourd'hui qu'on voit cette main parricide,   875
Des restes de ta vie insolemment avide,
Vouloir encor percer ce sein infortuné,
Pour y chercher le cœur que tu m'avais donné,
De la paix qu'elle rompt je ne suis plus le gage,
Je brise avec honneur mon illustre esclavage,   880
J'ose reprendre un cœur pour aimer et haïr,
Et ce n'est plus qu'à toi que je veux obéir.
    Le consentiras-tu cet effort sur ma flamme,
Toi, son vivant portrait, que j'adore dans l'âme,
Cher Prince, dont je n'ose en mes plus doux souhaits   885
Fier encor le nom aux murs de ce palais?
Je sais quelles seront tes douleurs et tes craintes,
Je vois déjà tes maux, j'entends déjà tes plaintes,
Mais pardonne aux devoirs qu'exige enfin un roi
A qui tu dois le jour qu'il a perdu pour moi.   890
J'aurai mêmes douleurs, j'aurai mêmes alarmes;
S'il t'en coûte un soupir, j'en verserai des larmes.
    Mais, Dieux! que je me trouble en les voyant tous deux!
Amour, qui me confonds, cache du moins tes feux,
Et content de mon cœur dont je te fais le maître,   895
Dans mes regards surpris garde-toi de paraître.

chains of enforced neglect! Answer at last his cry for justice,
justice for the great king's ghost! Appear, let me see again
the bloodied form I saw before, when flashing with love
and wrath, all wounds, it cried, "Farewell, avenge me; I
die for you!" Alas, beloved ghost, I have not sought your
revenge. Was I not ready to kiss the very hand, and with a
daughter's respect, that stole your life, the very hand that
spilled your blood? But forgive me, these burdens are imposed by rank. The nearer our birth to the crown, the
greater our enslavement to greatness. Our hearts are not
for our loves, our hates; all our passions know obedience
alone. We armed ourselves to avenge this outrage; today I
am but the pledge to that ill-conceived truce, sacrificed on
the altar of state; eyes blind to the sacrilege, I follow a
predestined course. But today the parricidal hand is raised
and lusts for remnants of your heart's last blood; it will stab
this wretched breast, tear out the heart you set within.
Today I do with honor throw off my royal chains, free of
the pledge she has dishonored. I dare again leave my heart
to love and hate; and you alone I obey in all!

   But you, his living image, idol of my adoring soul: most
dear prince, whose name sweetest desire dares not speak
within these walls—do you consent, if I stifle thus my heart?
I know and I see, I hear already your complaint, your pain,
your sorrow, your fears. Forgive what I do, compelled by
the king to whom you owe the life he lost for me. My heart
will shudder with your alarms, mourn your sorrows; with
every sigh my eyes will shed your tears.

                 [*She sees the princes approach.*]

But Gods above! How I am undone when they appear!
Love, that confounds my soul, let at least your light be
hidden; be content, master of my heart alone; do not shine
from my unguarded eyes.

[III.iv]   Antiochus, Séleucus, Rodogune.

ANTIOCHUS.

Ne vous offensez pas, Princesse, de nous voir
De vos yeux à vous-même expliquer le pouvoir.
Ce n'est pas d'aujourd'hui que nos cœurs en soupirent;
A vos premiers regards tous deux ils se rendirent,   900
Mais un profond respect nous fit taire et brûler,
Et ce même respect nous force de parler.
    L'heureux moment approche où votre destinée
Semble être aucunement à la nôtre enchaînée,
Puisque d'un droit d'aînesse, incertain parmi nous,   905
La nôtre attend un sceptre et la vôtre un époux.
C'est trop d'indignité que notre souveraine
De l'un de ses captifs tienne le nom de reine.
Notre amour s'en offense, et changeant cette loi,
Remet à notre reine à nous choisir un roi.   910
Ne vous abaissez plus à suivre la couronne,
Donnez-la, sans souffrir qu'avec elle on vous donne,
Réglez notre destin, qu'ont mal réglé les Dieux;
Notre seul droit d'aînesse est de plaire à vos yeux.
L'ardeur qu'allume en nous une flamme si pure   915
Préfère votre choix au choix de la nature,
Et vient sacrifier à votre élection
Toute notre espérance et notre ambition.
    Prononcez donc, Madame, et faites un monarque.
Nous céderons sans honte à cette illustre marque,   920
Et celui qui perdra votre divin objet
Demeurera du moins votre premier sujet.
Son amour immortel saura toujours lui dire
Que ce rang près de vous vaut ailleurs un empire;
Il y mettra sa gloire, et dans un tel malheur,   925
L'heur de vous obéir flattera sa douleur.

RODOGUNE.

Princes, je dois beaucoup à cette déférence
De votre ambition et de votre espérance,
Et j'en recevrais l'offre avec quelque plaisir,
Si celles de mon rang avaient droit de choisir.   930
Comme sans leur avis les rois disposent d'elles,
Pour affermir leur trône ou finir leurs querelles,

[III.iv]   *Enter* Antiochus *and* Seleucus.

ANTIOCHUS.

Take no offense, princess, that we come to tell you how
your eyes command us. Day after day we have sighed for
them. We saw you, and as one we surrendered our hearts,
for they are yours. In deepest respect they have burned
silently, but now respect compels our speech.

The fortunate hour is near when your destiny it seems
must in some way be linked with ours, for while the rights
of an elder son stand undecided between us we are fated to
wait for a scepter, you a husband. But it wounds too deeply
our lady's sovereign dignity, that she will stand indebted to
captive suitors for the name of queen. The love we feel
would change that law, would restore to our queen her
choice of king. Stoop no more, waiting on the crown; it is
yours to give. Do not consent to be a gift with what is yours
to bestow. Command our destinies, that the Gods have so
ill commanded. The first prior right is to be pleasing in
your eyes. The pure, fervent passions burning here elect
your choice, not the choice of nature; we have come to
sacrifice our hope, our ambition—you must tell us how.

Pronounce our fate, madam; choose the monarch. We
surrender without shame or dishonor to that glorious sign,
for even he who loses your divine beauty remains no less
than first among your subjects. His eternal love can yet
boast in that title a higher honor than attends in another
land the emperor's crown. Therein lies his glory, and
though unfortunate in his loss, in the very pain he will find
great joy.

RODOGUNE.

Noble princes, the sacrifice of your ambition and hope is a
deference I would accept with pleasure indeed, if such
acceptance were lawful in women of my birth. But as kings
dispose of us, careless of our desire, to buttress a throne or
compose a quarrel, the fate of nations is our own as well;

Le destin des États est arbitre du leur,
Et l'ordre des traités règle tout dans leur cœur.
C'est lui que suit le mien, et non pas la couronne ;   935
J'aimerai l'un de vous, parce qu'il me l'ordonne.
Du secret révélé j'en prendrai le pouvoir,
Et mon amour pour naître attendra mon devoir.
N'attendez rien de plus, ou votre attente est vaine.
Le choix que vous m'offrez appartient à la Reine ;   940
J'entreprendrais sur elle à l'accepter de vous.
Peut-être on vous a tu jusqu'où va son courroux,
Mais je dois par épreuve assez bien le connaître
Pour fuir l'occasion de le faire renaître.
Que n'en ai-je souffert, et que n'a-t-elle osé ?   945
Je veux croire avec vous que tout est apaisé,
Mais craignez avec moi que ce choix ne ranime
Cette haine mourante à quelque nouveau crime.
Pardonnez-moi ce mot qui viole un oubli
Que la paix entre nous doit avoir établi.   950
Le feu qui semble éteint souvent dort sous la cendre :
Qui l'ose réveiller peut s'en laisser surprendre ;
Et je mériterais qu'il me pût consumer,
Si je lui fournissais de quoi se rallumer.

SÉLEUCUS.

Pouvez-vous redouter sa haine renaissante,   955
S'il est en votre main de la rendre impuissante ?
Faites un roi, Madame, et régnez avec lui.
Son courroux désarmé demeure sans appui,
Et toutes ses fureurs sans effet rallumées
Ne pousseront en l'air que de vaines fumées.   960
Mais a-t-elle intérêt au choix que vous ferez,
Pour en craindre les maux que vous vous figurez ?
La couronne est à nous, et sans lui faire injure,
Sans manquer de respect aux droits de la nature,
Chacun de nous à l'autre en peut céder sa part,   965
Et rendre à votre choix ce qu'il doit au hasard.
Qu'un si faible scrupule en notre faveur cesse :
Votre inclination vaut bien un droit d'aînesse
Dont vous seriez traitée avec trop de rigueur,
S'il se trouvait contraire aux vœux de votre cœur.   970
On vous applaudirait quand vous seriez à plaindre ;

the heart of a princess is ruled by treaty. By such my heart
is commanded, not by desire for a crown. I shall love one of
you; the treaty will have it so. My powers will come with
the revelation of that secret, and my love is waiting to be
born from that duty. Expect no more, or you will expect in
vain. It is the queen's choice you come to offer; but I would
usurp her right in taking it from another hand than hers.
Perhaps it has been disguised from you, how hotly burns
her wrath; but I, having felt the flames, know better than
to welcome occasions to stir it again. Is there a torture I
have not endured, is there an outrage she has not dared?
I hope with you that all is peace; but beware, as I do, lest
this very choice revive her dying hatred, urge her on to
another crime. Forgive me, such words violate the silence
our treaty has wrapped us in. A fire dies out, we think, but
slumbers beneath the ash; one who rekindles it can be
caught—and if I add new fuel, I am justly rewarded, if I
am consumed.

SELEUCUS.

But need you fear the rebirth of hate, if it lies in you to
destroy its power? Make one of us king, madam, and
reign by his side. Her wrath disarmed, all unsupported,
may flame again; it can but fill the air with harmless smoke.
Moreover, what does your choice matter to her, that you
fear these fancied disasters? The crown is ours; without
injury or disrespect to her natural claim, each of us can
surrender his share to the other, and restore to your choice
what once belonged to chance. Scruple no more on our
account; your favor is worth all the rights of prior birth,
which would treat you too harshly if they should run
counter to your heart's desire, bringing you reverence when
you had a right to pity. Thus to put the scepter in your

Pour vous faire régner, ce serait vous contraindre,
Vous donner la couronne en vous tyrannisant,
Et verser du poison sur ce noble présent.
Au nom de ce beau feu qui tous deux nous consume,   975
Princesse, à notre espoir ôtez cette amertume,
Et permettez que l'heur qui suivra votre époux
Se puisse redoubler à le tenir de vous.

RODOGUNE.

Ce beau feu vous aveugle autant comme il vous brûle,
Et, tâchant d'avancer, son effort vous recule.   980
Vous croyez que ce choix, que l'un et l'autre attend,
Pourra faire un heureux sans faire un mécontent,
Et moi, quelque vertu que votre cœur prépare,
Je crains d'en faire deux si le mien se déclare.
Non que de l'un et l'autre il dédaigne les vœux :   985
Je tiendrais à bonheur d'être à l'un de vous deux,
Mais souffrez que je suive enfin ce qu'on m'ordonne ;
Je me mettrai trop haut s'il faut que je me donne :
Quoique aisément je cède aux ordres de mon Roi,
Il n'est pas bien aisé de m'obtenir de moi.   990
Savez-vous quels devoirs, quels travaux, quels services
Voudront de mon orgueil exiger les caprices ?
Par quels degrès de gloire on me peut mériter ?
En quels affreux périls il faudra vous jeter ?
Ce cœur vous est acquis, après le diadème,   995
Princes, mais gardez-vous de le rendre à lui-même :
Vous y renoncerez peut- être pour jamais,
Quand je vous aurai dit à quel prix je le mets.

SÉLEUCUS.

Quels seront les devoirs, quels travaux, quels services
Dont nous ne vous fassions d'amoureux sacrifices,   1000
Et quels affreux périls pourrons-nous redouter,
Si c'est par ces degrés qu'on peut vous mériter ?

ANTIOCHUS.

Princesse, ouvrez ce cœur, et jugez mieux du nôtre,
Jugez mieux du beau feu qui brûle l'un et l'autre,
Et dites hautement à quel prix votre choix   1005
Veut faire l'un de nous le plus heureux des rois.

RODOGUNE.

Princes, le voulez-vous ?

hand would be too much constraint; to bestow the crown
in tyrannizing over you would poison the noble gift. In the
name of these pure fires that consume our hearts, princess,
purge our hope of this bitterness: let the good fortune
that follows your husband be doubled in receiving it from
you.

RODOGUNE.

That splendid fire blinds as it consumes you, and though
you may think it advances your hopes, by its force they are
driven back. You think that this choice long awaited by
both can make one joyful without discontent for the other,
and as for me, though you may strengthen your hearts, I
think both shall be discontent when the desire in mine is
known. I do not say it disdains the hopes of either. To be
yours—or yours, I should feel it a happiness. But allow me
to follow the orders I receive. I shall set my price too high,
if I am allowed to be mine to give. I surrender easily to the
command of my king, but it will not be easy to obtain me
from myself. Do you know what duty, what labors, what
services that in the pride of my caprice I shall demand?
What glorious heights must be scaled to win me? What
fearful dangers must be braved? My heart can be won
with the diadem, noble princes. Take care lest, returning
the crown to that heart, you renounce it perhaps forever
when I have told you the price I ask.

SELEUCUS.

What duties, what labors, what services would we not per-
form for love of you? What fearful dangers would daunt
us, if we can win your love on those glorious heights?

ANTIOCHUS.

Princess, open your heart, and think better of ours; esteem
more highly the ardent passions that consume us both, and
tell us plainly at what cost you intend to make one of us the
happiest of kings.

RODOGUNE.

That is your wish, noble princes?

ANTIOCHUS.   C'est notre unique envie.

RODOGUNE.

Je verrai cette ardeur d'un repentir suivie.

SÉLEUCUS.

Avant ce repentir, tous deux nous périrons.

RODOGUNE.

Enfin vous le voulez?

SÉLEUCUS.   Nous vous en conjurons.   1010

RODOGUNE.

Eh bien donc! il est temps de me faire connaître.
J'obéis à mon roi, puisqu'un de vous doit l'être,
Mais quand j'aurai parlé, si vous vous en plaignez,
J'atteste tous les Dieux que vous m'y contraignez,
Et que c'est malgré moi qu'à moi-même rendue   1015
J'écoute une chaleur qui m'était défendue,
Qu'un devoir rappelé me rend un souvenir
Que la foi des traités ne doit plus retenir.

Tremblez, Princes, tremblez au nom de votre père:
Il est mort, et pour moi, par les mains d'une mère.   1020
Je l'avais oublié, sujette à d'autres lois,
Mais libre, je lui rends enfin ce que je dois.
C'est à vous de choisir mon amour ou ma haine:
J'aime les fils du Roi, je hais ceux de la Reine.
Réglez-vous là-dessus, et sans plus me presser   1025
Voyez auquel des deux vous voulez renoncer.
Il faut prendre parti, mon choix suivra le vôtre:
Je respecte autant l'un que je déteste l'autre,
Mais ce que j'aime en vous du sang de ce grand roi,
S'il n'est digne de lui, n'est pas digne de moi.   1030
Ce sang que vous portez, ce trône qu'il vous laisse,
Valent bien que pour lui votre cœur s'intéresse:
Votre gloire le veut, l'amour vous le prescrit.
Qui peut contre elle et lui soulever votre esprit?
Si vous leur préférez une mère cruelle,   1035
Soyez cruels, ingrats, parricides comme elle.
Vous devez la punir, si vous la condamnez,
Vous devez l'imiter, si vous la soutenez.
Quoi? cette ardeur s'éteint! l'un et l'autre soupire!
J'avais su le prévoir, j'avais su le prédire . . .   1040

ANTIOCHUS.

We have no other.

RODOGUNE.

I shall see repentance follow hard upon this ardor.

SELEUCUS.

Sooner than repent, we would both die.

RODOGUNE.

For the last time, you wish me to—?

SELEUCUS.

We both implore you.

RODOGUNE.

Well, then! It is time that I make myself known. I obey my
king, since one of you it is to be. But when I have spoken,
if you complain, I call the Gods to witness, you have
forced me to this, that in spite of myself, I am myself again!
And I hear a passion that was forbidden to me. A duty
remembered brings back the memory that words of truce
must no longer restrain.

Tremble, princes, tremble at the name of your father.
He died, and for me, at a mother's hand. I had forgot him,
obedient to other laws. Today I am free and I discharge
my debt at last. It is for you to choose, my love or my
hate! I love the sons of that king; I hate the sons of the
queen. Set your course by that and urge me no further; it
is for you to say which parent you renounce. You must cast
your lot, and my choice will follow yours. I revere one as I
detest the other, but the blood of the great king which I
love in you, deserves ill of me if it is unworthy of him. His
blood in your veins, his throne left to you demands that
your hearts take up his cause. Your fame requires, love pre-
scribes that you do. In whose cause may your soul stand
against both love and fame? If your cruel mother is more to
you than they, be as cruel, ingrate, and as criminal as she.
You must, if you condemn, punish her. If you defend,
imitate her. Ah, that ardent love is quite extinguished.
Sighs from both? I foresaw, I said it would be so.

ANTIOCHUS.
    Princesse . . .
RODOGUNE.   Il n'est plus temps, le mot en est lâché.
    Quand j'ai voulu me taire, en vain je l'ai tâché.
    Appelez ce devoir haine, rigueur, colère:
    Pour gagner Rodogune il faut venger un père.
    Je me donne à ce prix. Osez me mériter,   1045
    Et voyez qui de vous daignera m'accepter.
    Adieu, Princes.

[III.v]   Antiochus *et* Séleucus.

ANTIOCHUS.   Hélas! c'est donc ainsi qu'on traite
    Les plus profonds respects d'une amour si parfaite!
SÉLEUCUS.
    Elle nous fuit, mon frère, après cette rigueur.
ANTIOCHUS.
    Elle fuit, mais en Parthe, en nous perçant le cœur.   1050
SÉLEUCUS.
    Que le ciel est injuste! Une âme si cruelle
    Méritait notre mère, et devait naître d'elle.
ANTIOCHUS.
    Plaignons-nous sans blasphème.
SÉLEUCUS.   Ah! que vous me gênez
    Par cette retenue où vous vous obstinez!
    Faut-il encor régner? faut-il l'aimer encore?   1055
ANTIOCHUS.
    Il faut plus de respect pour celle qu'on adore.
SÉLEUCUS.
    C'est ou d'elle ou du trône être ardemment épris,
    Que vouloir ou l'aimer ou régner à ce prix.
ANTIOCHUS.
    C'est et d'elle et de lui tenir bien peu de compte,
    Que faire une révolte et si pleine et si prompte.   1060
SÉLEUCUS.
    Lorsque l'obéissance a tant d'impiété,
    La révolte devient une nécessité.
ANTIOCHUS.
    La révolte, mon frère, est bien précipitée,
    Quand la loi qu'elle rompt peut être rétractée;

ANTIOCHUS.

Princess—

RODOGUNE.

The moment has passed; the words have been said. I
wanted to remain silent, but you would not permit me. Call
my duty hatred, my harshness, anger. To win Rodogune,
a father must be avenged. I am yours at that price; let us
see which of you will dare deserve me, deign to have me.
Farewell, princes.   *Exit* Rodogune.

[III.v]

ANTIOCHUS.

Ah, will she use thus our deepest reverence, our perfect
love!

SELEUCUS.

She flies from us after so harsh a blow.

ANTIOCHUS.

She flies like the Parthian, her arrows piercing our heart.

SELEUCUS.

Oh, injustice of Heaven, a soul so cruel deserved a mother
like ours; from that womb she ought to have come.

ANTIOCHUS.

Come, let us complain, but not with blasphemy.

SELEUCUS.

Ah, you also torture me, with your obstinate restraint.
Must we still reign? Must we love her still?

ANTIOCHUS.

We must respect the woman we adore.

SELEUCUS.

We long for the throne and her ardently indeed, if we want
love or a kingdom at that price.

ANTIOCHUS.

We hold her and it in little esteem, if we rebel in such
haste, in such full measure.

SELEUCUS.

If obedience is impious to that degree, revolt is then our
duty.

ANTIOCHUS.

It is too hasty a revolt, Seleucus, when the law it breaks

Et c'est à nos désirs trop de témérité   1065
De vouloir de tels biens avec facilité.
Le ciel par les travaux veut qu'on monte à la gloire;
Pour gagner un triomphe, il faut une victoire.
Mais que je tâche en vain de flatter nos tourments!
Nos malheurs sont plus forts que ces déguisements: 1070
Leur excès à mes yeux paraît un noir abîme
Où la haine s'apprête à couronner le crime,
Où la gloire est sans nom, la vertu sans honneur,
Où sans un parricide, il n'est point de bonheur,
Et voyant de ces maux l'épouvantable image,   1075
Je me sens affaiblir, quand je vous encourage:
Je frémis, je chancelle, et mon cœur abattu
Suit tantôt sa douleur, et tantôt sa vertu.
Mon frère, pardonnez à des discours sans suite
Qui font trop voir le trouble où mon âme est réduite.   1080

SÉLEUCUS.

J'en ferais comme vous, si mon esprit troublé
Ne secouait le joug dont il est accablé.
Dans mon ambition, dans l'ardeur de ma flamme,
Je vois ce qu'est un trône, et ce qu'est une femme;
Et jugeant par leur prix de leur possession,   1085
J'éteins enfin ma flamme, et mon ambition.
Et je vous céderais l'un et l'autre avec joie,
Si dans la liberté que le ciel me renvoie,
La crainte de vous faire un funeste présent
Ne me jetait dans l'âme un remords trop cuisant.   1090
    Dérobons-nous, mon frère, à ces âmes cruelles,
Et laissons-les sans nous achever leurs querelles.

ANTIOCHUS.

Comme j'aime beaucoup, j'espère encore un peu.
L'espoir ne peut s'éteindre où brûle tant de feu,
Et son reste confus me rend quelques lumières   1095
Pour juger mieux que vous de ces âmes si fières.
Croyez-moi, l'une et l'autre a redouté nos pleurs:
Leur fuite à nos soupirs a dérobé leurs cœurs,
Et si tantôt leur haine eût attendu nos larmes,
Leur haine à nos douleurs aurait rendu les armes.   1100

SÉLEUCUS.

Pleurez donc à leurs yeux, gémissez, soupirez,

may itself be revoked. Our desires are much too bold, if we
expect rewards to come with ease. By Heaven's will, glory
is won by arduous labors. A triumphal march is earned by
victories won. But in vain I try to soothe the torment! Our
misfortunes are too heavy to be disguised. In their excess I
see a dark abyss, where hatred prepares a crown for crime,
where glory is nameless, virtue the loss of honor, where
only parricides can live at ease. At this frightful image of
evil I am overcome even as I encourage you. I shudder,
grow faint with terror—and my heart disheartened, halts
with its pain, revives with its courage. Brother, forgive this
incoherent speech; it shows too well the confusion in which
my soul is drowning.

SELEUCUS.

I would speak as you do, if my troubled mind did not throw
off the strangling yoke. Though I feel ambition, and the
force of love, I see what the throne is, what a woman is; and
judging their worth by what they will cost before we possess them, I extinguish the fires of love and my ambition.
I would surrender both to you, joyfully, did I not fear, in
my heaven-granted freedom, that it would be a fatal gift,
and a source of burning remorse to me.

Let us escape from these cruel furies, brother; let them
end their quarrels without us.

ANTIOCHUS.

As my love is great, I have yet a little hope. It cannot die
where fires burn so bright, and in the last flickering rays I
see, better than you, their proud spirit. Believe me, they
both dreaded to see us weep; they fled to steal their hearts
from our sighs, for if, just now, hatred had paused to see
that we wept, hatred would have laid down its arms before
our woes.

SELEUCUS.

Then weep before their very eyes; loose your groans, your

Et je craindrai pour vous ce que vous espérez.
Quoi qu'en votre faveur vos pleurs obtiennent d'elles,
Il vous faudra parer leurs haines mutuelles,
Sauver l'une de l'autre, et peut-être leurs coups,   1105
Vous trouvant au milieu, ne perceront que vous.
C'est ce qu'il faut pleurer. Ni maîtresse ni mère
N'ont plus de choix ici ni de lois à nous faire :
Quoi que leur rage exige, ou de vous ou de moi,
Rodogune est à vous, puisque je vous fais Roi.   1110
Épargnez vos soupirs près de l'une et de l'autre,
J'ai trouvé mon bonheur, saisissez-vous du vôtre ;
Je n'en suis point jaloux, et ma triste amitié
Ne le verra jamais que d'un œil de pitié.

[III.vi]   Antiochus.

ANTIOCHUS.

Que je serais heureux, si je n'aimais un frère !   1115
Lorsqu'il ne veut pas voir le mal qu'il se veut faire,
Mon amitié s'oppose à son aveuglement :
Elle agira pour vous, mon frère, également,
Et n'abusera point de cette violence
Que l'indignation fait à votre espérance.   1120
La pesanteur du coup souvent nous étourdit,
On le croit repoussé quand il s'approfondit,
Et quoi qu'un juste orgueil sur l'heure persuade,
Qui ne sent point son mal est d'autant plus malade :
Ces ombres de santé cachent mille poisons,   1125
Et la mort suit de près ces fausses guérisons.
Daignent les justes Dieux rendre vain ce présage !
Cependant allons voir si nous vaincrons l'orage,
Et si contre l'effort d'un si puissant courroux
La nature, et l'amour voudront parler pour nous.   1130

Fin du troisième acte.

sighs, and what you hope is still my fear. For you, they may give what your tears demand, but you must yet be on guard against that mutual hate, you must save one from the other; and perhaps their thrusts will go home in you, while you stand between. That is what I shall have to weep over. Neither our beloved nor our mother has any longer to command here, nor laws to lay down for us. In their rage, they may order as they please; Rodogune is yours, for I make you king. Whether with one or the other, save your laments. I have found my happiness, grasp your own. I have no envy. My saddened affection will always be looking with eyes of pity. *Exit* Seleucus.

[III.vi]

ANTIOCHUS.

How happy would I be, but for loving such a brother. Since he will not see how he wounds himself, my love must struggle with his blindness. I shall work in your behalf, brother, as in my own, and make no abuse of the violence you do your hopes in indignation.

Often we are stunned by the sheer weight of a blow, and in our bewilderment we believe we parried it well when we are most deeply struck. And though pride in our strength will convince us for a moment that all is well, though we feel no pain, we are all the more stricken. These shows of health conceal a thousand poisons, and death soon follows the false recovery. May the Gods, in their justice, show my foreboding is vain. For now, let us see how we may last out the storm, how nature and love may speak for us in the teeth of this wrath.

End of the Third Act.

ACTE IV

Antiochus *et* Rodogune.

RODOGUNE.

Prince, qu'ai-je entendu? parce que je soupire,
Vous présumez que j'aime, et vous m'osez le dire!
Est-ce un frère, est-ce vous dont la témérité
S'imagine . . .

ANTIOCHUS. Apaisez ce courage irrité,
Princesse, aucun de nous ne serait téméraire   1135
Jusqu'à s'imaginer qu'il eût l'heur de vous plaire.
Je vois votre mérite et le peu que je vaux,
Et ce rival si cher connaît mieux ses défauts.
Mais si tantôt ce cœur parlait par votre bouche,
Il veut que nous croyions qu'un peu d'amour le touche,   1140
Et qu'il daigne écouter quelques-uns de nos vœux,
Puisqu'il tient à bonheur d'être à l'un de nous deux.
Si c'est présomption de croire ce miracle,
C'est une impiété de douter de l'oracle,
Et mériter les maux où vous nous condamnez,   1145
Qu'éteindre un bel espoir que vous nous ordonnez.
Princesse, au nom des Dieux, au nom de cette flamme . . .

RODOGUNE.

Un mot ne fait pas voir jusques au fond d'une âme,
Et votre espoir trop prompt prend trop de vanité
Des termes obligeants de ma civilité.   1150
Je l'ai dit, il est vrai, mais quoi qu'il en puisse être,
Méritez cet amour que vous voulez connaître.
Lorsque j'ai soupiré, ce n'était pas pour vous,
J'ai donné ces soupirs aux mânes d'un époux;
Et ce sont les effets du souvenir fidèle   1155
Que sa mort à toute heure en mon âme rappelle.
Princes, soyez ses fils, et prenez son parti.

ANTIOCHUS.

Recevez donc son cœur en nous deux réparti:
Ce cœur qu'un saint amour rangea sous votre empire,
Ce cœur pour qui le vôtre à tous moments soupire,   1160

ACT IV

[IV.i]   Antiochus *and* Rodogune.

RODOGUNE.

Prince, what do I hear? Because I sigh, you presume it is
love—and you dare tell me so? Do you or your brother
have the temerity to imagine—

ANTIOCHUS.

Do not be offended, princess, I beg you. Neither of us
would be so rash as to imagine himself so fortunate as to
enjoy your favor: I see your worth and my own small merit,
and my brother, my rival, knows better his faults. But if
just now your lips spoke words of the heart, it must wish us
to believe that love has touched it slightly at least, and that
it will deign to hear our pleas, since it envisages happiness
in belonging to one of us. Is it presumptuous to believe in
that miracle? For it would be impious to doubt the oracle,
and we should deserve the woes you condemn us to if we
stifled the bright hope we entertain at your behest. In the
God's name, princess, in the name of that love—

RODOGUNE.

One word alone cannot illuminate the depths of a soul; and
your hope feeds its vanity too soon on kind, courteous
phrases. True, I have said that word, but then: you must
earn the love you wish to discover. When I sighed, it was
not for you, but for the spirit of my betrothed; I sighed for
memories constantly stirred in my faithful soul by his
death. Princes, be his sons, take his part.

ANTIOCHUS.

Accept then his heart, shared by his sons. Accept this
heart brought by holy love under your rule! This heart

Ce cœur en vous aimant indignement percé
Reprend pour vous aimer le sang qu'il a versé.
Il le reprend en nous, il revit, il vous aime,
Et montre, en vous aimant, qu'il est encor le même.
Ah! Princesse, en l'état où le sort nous a mis,   1165
Pouvons-nous mieux montrer que nous sommes ses fils?

RODOGUNE.

Si c'est son cœur en vous qui revit, et qui m'aime,
Faites ce qu'il ferait s'il vivait en lui-même.
A ce cœur qu'il vous laisse osez prêter un bras;
Pouvez-vous le porter et ne l'écouter pas?   1170
S'il vous explique mal ce qu'il en doit attendre,
Il emprunte ma voix pour se mieux faire entendre.
Une seconde fois il vous le dit par moi:
Prince, il faut le venger.

ANTIOCHUS.   J'accepte cette loi.
Nommez les assassins, et j'y cours.

RODOGUNE.   Quel mystère   1175
Vous fait, en l'acceptant, méconnaître une mère?

ANTIOCHUS.

Ah! si vous ne voulez voir finir nos destins,
Nommez d'autres vengeurs ou d'autres assassins.

RODOGUNE.

Ah! je vois trop régner son parti dans votre âme,
Prince, vous le prenez.

ANTIOCHUS.   Oui, je le prends, Madame,   1180
Et j'apporte à vos pieds le plus pur de son sang,
Que la nature enferme en ce malheureux flanc.
    Satisfaites vous-même à cette voix secrète
Dont la vôtre envers nous daigne être l'interprète,
Exécutez son ordre, et hâtez-vous sur moi   1185
De punir une Reine et de venger un Roi:
Mais quitte par ma mort d'un devoir si sévère,
Écoutez-en un autre en faveur de mon frère.
De deux Princes unis à soupirer pour vous.
Prenez l'un pour victime et l'autre pour époux.   1190
Punissez un des fils des crimes de la mère,
Mais payez l'autre aussi des services du père,
Et laissez un exemple à la postérité
Et de rigueur entière et d'entière équité.

that sighs at every moment for yours! This heart, foully
stabbed as loving you it beat, fills again, to love you, with the
blood it lost; feeding at our veins, it lives again and loves
you still, and proves itself, loving you, still the same. Ah,
princess, in the condition destiny has ordained for us, can
we better prove ourselves his sons?

RODOGUNE.

If his heart lives in you and loves me still, do then what it
would do, if it lived in his own breast! Lend arms to the
heart he bequeathed to you, do you dare? Can your breast
contain it, yet not hear its beat? If it has said unclearly
what it must want from you, it borrows my voice so you
will better understand. A second time it summons you,
through me: prince, he must be avenged.

ANTIOCHUS.

I accept that law: name the assassins, and I strike!

RODOGUNE.

Accepting this law, for what mysterious cause do you not
recognize your mother's guilt?

ANTIOCHUS.

Ah! Unless you wish to hasten our end, name other aven-
gers, or other assassins.

RODOGUNE.

Ah! I see your soul is swayed too much by her concerns.
Prince, you take her part!

ANTIOCHUS.

Yes, madam, I do, and it is the best part, her purest blood,
that Nature made flow in these wretched veins.

With your own hand, appease that secret voice yours has
deigned to let speak to us. Obey its command, let your
blows fall upon me to punish a queen, avenge a king. But
relieved of stern duty by my death, hear another voice, for
my brother's sake. Of the two princes, adoring you as one,
let the first be your victim, the other your husband.
Punish a son for the crime of his mother, but reward the
other for his father's love; and leave for all time examples
of justice most strict and of the strictest equity! Well then?
Do you hear neither love nor hate? Will I be granted

Quoi ? n'écouterez-vous ni l'amour ni la haine ?   1195
Ne pourrai-je obtenir ni salaire ni peine ?
Ce cœur qui vous adore, et que vous dédaignez . . .
RODOGUNE.
Hélas ! Prince.
ANTIOCHUS.   Est-ce encor le Roi que vous plaignez ?
Ce soupir ne va-t-il que vers l'ombre d'un père ?
RODOGUNE.
Allez, ou pour le moins rappelez votre frère.   1200
Le combat pour mon âme était moins dangereux
Lorsque je vous avais à combattre tous deux.
Vous êtes plus fort seul que vous n'étiez ensemble ;
Je vous bravais tantôt, et maintenant je tremble.
J'aime ; n'abusez pas, Prince, de mon secret.   1205
Au milieu de ma haine il m'échappe à regret,
Mais enfin il m'échappe, et cette retenue
Ne peut plus soutenir l'effort de votre vue.
Oui, j'aime un de vous deux malgré ce grand courroux,
Et ce dernier soupir dit assez que c'est vous.   1210
    Un rigoureux devoir à cet amour s'oppose.
Ne m'en accusez point, vous en êtes la cause,
Vous l'avez fait renaître en me pressant d'un choix
Qui rompt de vos traités les favorables lois.
D'un père mort pour moi voyez le sort étrange :   1215
Si vous me laissez libre, il faut que je le venge,
Et mes feux dans mon âme ont beau s'en mutiner,
Ce n'est qu'à ce prix seul que je puis me donner ;
Mais ce n'est pas de vous qu'il faut que je l'attende.
Votre refus est juste autant que ma demande ;   1220
A force de respect votre amour s'est trahi.
Je voudrais vous haïr s'il m'avait obéi,
Et je n'estime pas l'honneur d'une vengeance
Jusqu'à vouloir d'un crime être la récompense.
Rentrons donc sous les lois que m'impose la paix,   1225
Puisque m'en affranchir c'est vous perdre à jamais.
Prince, en votre faveur je ne puis davantage :
L'orgueil de ma naissance enfle encor mon courage,
Et quelque grand pouvoir que l'amour ait sur moi,
Je n'oublierai jamais que je me dois un roi.   1230
Oui, malgré mon amour, j'attendrai d'une mère

neither punishment nor reward? My heart that adores you,
that you spurn—

RODOGUNE.

Oh, prince!

ANTIOCHUS.

Is it still the king you pity? Are your sighs only for the
ghost of the father?

RODOGUNE.

No, you must leave me, or at least recall your brother. The
struggle in my soul was less perilous when I had you both
to combat. Alone you are stronger than you were together.
I could stand against you then. Now, I am trembling—I do
love. But use my secret fairly, prince. In the flood of hatred,
it slips from me. I regret it, but at last, it escapes, and my
reserve can no longer bear the strain of seeing you. Yes, I
love one of you, and this last sigh shows well enough, it is
you.

A stern duty opposes this love. Do not accuse me, you
are the cause. You brought it to life again when you urged
on me a choice, breaking the gentler terms of your treaty.
See how strange, the fate of the father who died for me: if
you set me free, I must avenge him, and the ardent love of
my heart mutinies in vain. Only at such a price can I give
my hand. But it is not by you I should expect to see it paid.
Your refusal is quite as just as my demand. In its deference
your love betrayed itself, but I should hate you if your
love had obeyed. Nor do I prize the honor of vengeance so
highly that I wish to be the spoils of a crime. Then let us
again observe the restrictions imposed on me by the
treaty, since if I throw them off I lose you forever. Prince,
even for you I can do no more. The pride of blood swells in
my heart always, and however great love's power, I can
never forget that a king is what I owe to myself. Yes, despite my love, I shall wait until by a mother's word the
throne gives me either your brother or you. While we wait

Que le trône me donne ou vous ou votre frère.
Attendant son secret, vous aurez mes désirs,
Et s'il le fait régner, vous aurez mes soupirs.
C'est tout ce qu'à mes feux ma gloire peut permettre,   1235
Et tout ce qu'à vos feux les miens osent promettre.

ANTIOCHUS.

Que voudrais-je de plus? son bonheur est le mien.
Rendez heureux ce frère, et je ne perdrai rien.
L'amitié le consent, si l'amour l'appréhende,
Je bénirai le ciel d'une perte si grande,   1240
Et quittant les douceurs de cet espoir flottant,
Je mourrai de douleur, mais je mourrai content.

RODOGUNE.

Et moi, si mon destin entre ses mains me livre,
Pour un autre que vous s'il m'ordonne de vivre,
Mon amour . . . Mais adieu, mon esprit se confond.   1245
Prince, si votre flamme à la mienne répond,
Si vous n'êtes ingrat à ce cœur qui vous aime,
Ne me revoyez point qu'avec le diadème.

[IV.ii]   Antiochus.

ANTIOCHUS.

Les plus doux de mes vœux enfin sont exaucés:
Tu viens de vaincre, amour, mais ce n'est pas assez.   1250
Si tu veux triompher en cette conjoncture,
Après avoir vaincu, fais vaincre la nature,
Et prête-lui pour nous ces tendres sentiments
Que ton ardeur inspire aux cœurs des vrais amants,
Cette pitié que force, et ces dignes faiblesses   1255
Dont la vigueur détruit les fureurs vengeresses.
Voici la Reine. Amour, nature, justes Dieux,
Faites-la-moi fléchir ou mourir à ses yeux.

[IV.iii]   Cléopâtre, Antiochus, Laonice.

CLÉOPÂTRE.

Eh bien! Antiochus, vous dois-je la couronne?

ANTIOCHUS.

Madame, vous savez si le ciel me la donne.   1260

on that secret, you have my desires; and after, if the secret
is that he shall reign, you will have my regrets. More than
that honor cannot permit; more than that my love dares
not promise you.

ANTIOCHUS.

What more could I ask? His happiness is also mine. Make
my brother happy, and I lose nothing. My love for him
consents, though love for you fills me with dread. I can
offer thanks to Heaven for such heavy loss. If I must
abandon these sweet, unsettled hopes, I shall die of the
pain, but die content.

RODOGUNE.

And I, if my fate is to be his, if I am commanded to live for
any other than you, my love—no, farewell. My mind is
too troubled. Prince, if your heart answers mine, if you are
not ungrateful that you are loved, do not see me again—
except with the crown.   *Exit* Rodogune.

[IV.ii]   Antiochus *alone*.

ANTIOCHUS.

My sweetest desire is at last fulfilled! Love, the victory is
yours! But it is not enough; if you would enjoy triumph
now, with victory won, now be victorious with Nature, and
lend her for our sake the tenderer feelings your fires ignite
in true lovers' hearts; inspire a pity that enforces silence,
inspire a noble weakness whose strength will destroy the
vengeful furies. —Here is the queen. Love, Nature, just
Gods! Ordain that she bend to me—or that I die before her
eyes!

[IV.iii]   *Enter* Cleopatra *and* Laonice.

CLEOPATRA.

Well, Antiochus! Do I owe you the crown?

ANTIOCHUS.

Madam, you know whether Heaven gives it to me.

CLÉOPÂTRE.

Vous savez mieux que moi si vous la méritez.

ANTIOCHUS.

Je sais que je péris si vous ne m'écoutez.

CLÉOPÂTRE.

Un peu trop lent peut-être à servir ma colère
Vous vous êtes laissé prévenir par un frère?
Il a su me venger quand vous délibériez,   1265
Et je dois à son bras ce que vous espériez?
Je vous en plains, mon fils, ce malheur est extrême:
C'est périr en effet que perdre un diadème.
Je n'y sais qu'un remède; encore est-il fâcheux,
Étonnant, incertain, et triste pour tous deux.   1270
Je périrai moi-même avant que de le dire,
Mais enfin on perd tout quand on perd un empire.

ANTIOCHUS.

Le remède à nos maux est tout en votre main,
Et n'a rien de fâcheux, d'étonnant, d'incertain;
Votre seule colère a fait notre infortune.   1275
Nous perdons tout, Madame, en perdant Rodogune.
Nous l'adorons tous deux; jugez en quels tourments
Nous jette la rigueur de vos commandements.
L'aveu de cet amour sans doute vous offense,
Mais enfin nos malheurs croissent par le silence,   1280
Et votre cœur, qu'aveugle un peu d'inimitié,
S'il ignore nos maux, n'en peut prendre pitié:
Au point où je les vois, c'en est le seul remède.

CLÉOPÂTRE.

Quelle aveugle fureur vous-même vous possède?
Avez-vous oublié que vous parlez à moi,   1285
Ou si vous présumez être déjà mon roi?

ANTIOCHUS.

Je tâche avec respect à vous faire connaître
Les forces d'un amour que vous avez fait naître.

CLÉOPÂTRE.

Moi, j'aurais allumé cet insolent amour?

ANTIOCHUS.

Et quel autre prétexte a fait notre retour?   1290
Nous avez-vous mandés qu'afin qu'un droit d'aînesse
Donnât à l'un de nous le trône et la Princesse?

CLEOPATRA.

You know more than I whether you deserve it.

ANTIOCHUS.

I know I perish if you do not listen to me.

CLEOPATRA.

Perhaps a little too slow to serve my anger, and you have let a brother forestall you? He could avenge me while you deliberated, and I owe his hand what you hoped for? I pity you, my son, for that is a great misfortune. To lose the diadem is death indeed. I know of only one remedy, and even that is painful, astonishing, uncertain, and sad for both of you. But then in the loss of an empire you lose everything.

ANTIOCHUS.

The remedy of our ills lies wholly with you. There is nothing painful, astonishing, uncertain in it. Your wrath is our only misfortune. We lose everything, madam, in losing Rodogune. We adore her both. Consider how your harsh command torments us.

The confession of this love offends you, no doubt, but our misfortunes feed on silence, and your heart, blind in its enmity, unless it knows our pain, cannot feel pity. And at this point, that is the only remedy I see.

CLEOPATRA.

And what blind fury possesses you yourself? Do you forget that you are speaking to me? Or do you presume to be king already?

ANTIOCHUS.

I try in all respect to acquaint you with the strength of a love that you yourself caused to exist.

CLEOPATRA.

You say that I kindled this insolent love?

ANTIOCHUS.

And what other pretext was there for bringing us home? Did you not summon us so that priority of birth might give one of us both throne and princess? More than that, you

Vous avez bien fait plus, vous nous l'avez fait voir
Et c'était par vos mains nous mettre en son pouvoir.
Qui de nous deux, Madame, eût osé s'en défendre,   1295
Quand vous nous ordonniez à tous deux d'y prétendre ?
Si sa beauté dès lors n'eût allumé nos feux,
Le devoir auprès d'elle eût attaché nos vœux ;
Le désir de régner eût fait la même chose,
Et dans l'ordre des lois que la paix nous impose,   1300
Nous devions aspirer à sa possession
Par amour, par devoir, ou par ambition.
Nous avons donc aimé, nous avons cru vous plaire.
Chacun de nous n'a craint que le bonheur d'un frère,
Et cette crainte enfin cédant à l'amitié,   1305
J'implore pour tous deux un moment de pitié.
Avons-nous dû prévoir cette haine cachée,
Que la foi des traités n'avait point arrachée ?

CLÉOPÂTRE.

Non, mais vous avez dû garder le souvenir
Des hontes que pour vous j'avais su prévenir,   1310
Et de l'indigne état où votre Rodogune
Sans moi, sans mon courage, eût mis votre fortune.
Je croyais que vos cœurs sensibles à ces coups
En sauraient conserver un généreux courroux,
Et je le retenais avec ma douceur feinte,   1315
Afin que grossissant sous un peu de contrainte,
Ce torrent de colère et de ressentiment
Fût plus impétueux en son débordement.
Je fais plus maintenant : je presse, sollicite,
Je commande, menace, et rien ne vous irrite.   1320
Le sceptre, dont ma main vous doit récompenser,
N'a point de quoi vous faire un moment balancer ;
Vous ne considérez ni lui, ni mon injure,
L'amour étouffe en vous la voix de la nature,
Et je pourrais aimer des fils dénaturés !   1325

ANTIOCHUS.

La nature et l'amour ont leurs droits séparés ;
L'un n'ôte point à l'autre une âme qu'il possède.

CLÉOPÂTRE.

Non, non, où l'amour règne il faut que l'autre cède.

showed her to us and with your very hands put us in her power. Which of us dared hold back, when you ordered both to claim her hand? From that moment, had her beauty not stirred our loves, duty would have fastened our hopes on her. The desire to reign would have done the same, and terms of the treaty command us to possess her, for love's sake, for duty, or for ambition. So we loved and thought it was to please you. Each of us dreaded only the good fortune of his brother, and that fear giving way at last to affection, I implore you for both, surrender a moment to pity. Ought we to have foreseen this masked hatred that oaths of peace had not uprooted?

CLEOPATRA.

No, but you should have remembered the shame I was able to spare you, the depths to which your fortunes would have fallen, because of your Rodogune, but for me, but for my courage. I thought your hearts, still sensitive to those shocks, would have nourished a noble wrath; and I was holding it in check, with my feigned softness, so that grown stronger by restraint, the torrent of anger and resentment would overflow more impetuously. Now I do more: I urge, beseech, command, threaten! But nothing rouses you. The scepter, the recompense due from my hand, has no power to sway you for an instant. You regard neither it nor my wrongs. Nature's voice is stifled in you by love. And I could love sons so unnatural!

ANTIOCHUS.

Nature and love have their different rights. A soul possessed by one is not taken from the other.

CLEOPATRA.

No, no! Where love holds sway, the other must give ground!

ANTIOCHUS.

    Leurs charmes à nos cœurs sont également doux.
Nous périrons tous deux s'il faut périr pour vous;   1330
Mais aussi . . .

CLÉOPÂTRE.   Poursuivez, fils ingrat et rebelle.

ANTIOCHUS.

    Nous périrons tous deux, s'il faut périr pour elle.

CLÉOPÂTRE.

    Périssez, périssez! Votre rébellion
Mérite plus d'horreur que de compassion.
Mes yeux sauront le voir sans verser une larme,   1335
Sans regarder en vous que l'objet qui vous charme,
Et je triompherai, voyant périr mes fils,
De ses adorateurs et de mes ennemis.

ANTIOCHUS.

    Eh bien! triomphez-en, que rien ne vous retienne.
Votre main tremble-t-elle? y voulez-vous la mienne?   1340
Madame, commandez, je suis prêt d'obéir:
Je percerai ce cœur qui vous ose trahir,
Heureux si par ma mort je puis vous satisfaire,
Et noyer dans mon sang toute votre colère!
Mais si la dureté de votre aversion   1345
Nomme encor notre amour une rébellion,
Du moins souvenez-vous qu'elle n'a pris pour armes
Que de faibles soupirs et d'impuissantes larmes.

CLÉOPÂTRE.

    Ah! que n'a-t-elle pris et la flamme et le fer!
Que bien plus aisément j'en saurais triompher!   1350
Vos larmes dans mon cœur ont trop d'intelligence;
Elles ont presque éteint cette ardeur de vengeance,
Je ne puis refuser des soupirs à vos pleurs,
Je sens que je suis mère auprès de vos douleurs.
C'en est fait, je me rends, et ma colère expire: 1355
Rodogune est à vous aussi bien que l'empire.
Rendez grâces aux Dieux qui vous ont fait l'aîné,
Possédez-la, régnez.

ANTIOCHUS.   Oh! moment fortuné!

    Oh! trop heureuse fin de l'excès de ma peine!
Je rends grâces aux Dieux qui calment votre haine.   1360
Madame, est-il possible?

ANTIOCHUS.

They draw our hearts with equal force. We shall die, if die
we must, for you; but also—

CLEOPATRA.

Go on, thankless, rebellious son.

ANTIOCHUS.

We shall die, if die we must for her.

CLEOPATRA.

Then die! Die! Your rebellion more deserves horror than
compassion. My eyes can look on and shed no tear, seeing
in you only that woman who binds you with her spells. And
I shall triumph, as I watch my sons die, over her lovers and
my enemies!

ANTIOCHUS.

Well then, triumph, let nothing hold you back! Does your
hand tremble? Shall I bring mine to steady it? Madam,
command me; I am ready to obey. I shall pierce the heart
that dares betray you, and happily if by my death I can
satisfy you and in my blood drown your anger. But if in
your harsh aversion you still call our love treason, remember at least that its only weapons have been weak sighs,
powerless tears.

CLEOPATRA.

Ah! Why did it not wield sword and flame! How easily
then could I triumph. Your tears speak only too well to my
heart. They almost put out the burning desire of vengeance.
I cannot refuse to sigh in answer to your weeping; I am a
mother when I see you in pain. It is over, I must yield; my
wrath expires. Take Rodogune and the empire as well;
they are yours. And be grateful to the Gods who made you
the elder.

ANTIOCHUS.

Oh, fortunate hour! My boundless pain is crowned with
excess of joy! I thank the Gods who appease your hatred.
Can this be true, madam?

CLÉOPÂTRE.   En vain j'ai résisté,
La nature est trop forte, et mon cœur s'est dompté.
Je ne vous dis plus rien, vous aimez votre mère,
Et votre amour pour moi taira ce qu'il faut taire.

ANTIOCHUS.
Quoi, je triomphe donc sur le point de périr!   1365
La main qui me blessait a daigné me guérir!

CLÉOPÂTRE.
Oui, je veux couronner une flamme si belle.
Allez à la Princesse en porter la nouvelle;
Son cœur, comme le vôtre, en deviendra charmé:
Vous n'aimeriez pas tant si vous n'étiez aimé.   1370

ANTIOCHUS.
Heureux Antiochus! heureuse Rodogune!
Oui, Madame, entre nous la joie en est commune.

CLÉOPÂTRE.
Allez donc, ce qu'ici vous perdez de moments
Sont autant de larcins à vos contentements,
Et ce soir, destiné pour la cérémonie,   1375
Fera voir pleinement si ma haine est finie.

ANTIOCHUS.
Et nous vous ferons voir tous nos désirs bornés
A vous donner en nous des sujets couronnés.

[IV.iv]   Cléopâtre *et* Laonice.

LAONICE.
Enfin ce grand courage a vaincu sa colère.

CLÉOPÂTRE.
Que ne peut point un fils sur le cœur d'une mère?   1380

LAONICE.
Vos pleurs coulent encore, et ce cœur adouci . . .

CLÉOPÂTRE.
Envoyez-moi son frère, et nous laissez ici.
Sa douleur sera grande, à ce que je présume,
Mais j'en saurai sur l'heure adoucir l'amertume.
Ne lui témoignez rien, il lui sera plus doux   1385
D'apprendre tout de moi, qu'il ne serait de vous.

CLEOPATRA.

It was vain to resist. Nature is too strong, and my heart is tamed. I shall say no more to you; you do love your mother, and that love shall silence what must be silenced.

ANTIOCHUS.

Is it possible, at the point of death I triumph? The hand that struck has bent to heal?

CLEOPATRA.

Yes, I would crown a love so beautiful. Go now to the princess and let her know. Her heart will be as delighted as yours, for you would not love so deeply if you were not loved.

ANTIOCHUS.

Happy Antiochus! Happy Rodogune! Yes, Mother, we share a mutual joy.

CLEOPATRA.

Then go; every moment wasted here is stolen from your happiness. And this evening, chosen for the ceremony, will remove every doubt whether my hatred is done.

ANTIOCHUS.

And we shall fully prove that our every desire is only to show you in us your crowned subjects.   *Exit* Antiochus.

[IV.iv]   *Enter* Laonice.

LAONICE.

So a magnanimous heart has at last conquered her wrath.

CLEOPATRA.

What can sons not do with a mother's heart?

LAONICE.

Your tears still flow; your softened heart—

CLEOPATRA.

Send his brother to me, and leave us. His sorrow will be great; at least so I presume, but I shall know how to soften the bitterness. Give him no hint; it will be easier if he learns everything from me, than if it were from you.

                                        Exit Laonice.

[IV.v]   Cléopâtre.

CLÉOPÂTRE.

Que tu pénètres mal le fond de mon courage!
Si je verse des pleurs, ce sont des pleurs de rage,
Et ma haine qu'en vain tu crois s'évanouir
Ne les a fait couler qu'afin de t'éblouir.   1390
Je ne veux plus que moi dedans ma confidence.
Et toi, crédule amant, que charme l'apparence,
Et dont l'esprit léger s'attache avidement
Aux attraits captieux de mon déguisement,
Va, triomphe en idée avec ta Rodogune,   1395
Au sort des immortels préfère ta fortune,
Tandis que mieux instruite en l'art de me venger,
En de nouveaux malheurs je saurai te plonger.
Ce n'est pas tout d'un coup que tant d'orgueil trébuche;
De qui se rend trop tôt on doit craindre une embûche,   1400
Et c'est mal démêler le cœur d'avec le front,
Que prendre pour sincère un changement si prompt.
L'effet te fera voir comme je suis changée.

[IV.vi]   Cléopâtre *et* Séleucus.

CLÉOPÂTRE.

Savez-vous, Séleucus, que je me suis vengée?
SÉLEUCUS.

Pauvre princesse, hélas!
CLÉOPÂTRE.   Vous déplorez son sort!   1405
Quoi? l'aimiez-vous?
SÉLEUCUS.   Assez pour regretter sa mort.
CLÉOPÂTRE.

Vous lui pouvez servir encor d'amant fidèle;
Si j'ai su me venger, ce n'a pas été d'elle.
SÉLEUCUS.

Oh ciel! et de qui donc, Madame?
CLÉOPÂTRE.   C'est de vous,
Ingrat, qui n'aspirez qu'à vous voir son époux,   1410
De vous, qui l'adorez en dépit d'une mère,
De vous, qui dédaignez de servir ma colère,
De vous, de qui l'amour, rebelle à mes désirs,
S'oppose à ma vengeance, et détruit mes plaisirs.

[IV.v]   Cleopatra *alone*.

CLEOPATRA.

You see but poorly into the depths of my heart! If my tears flow, they are tears of rage! And the hatred you vainly think dissolved made them flow only to blind your eyes. I will no longer trust anyone but myself. And you, gullible lover, entranced with false shows, your shallow mind grasping avidly at the deceptive lure of my mask, go play, you and your Rodogune, with your visions of triumph. Think yourselves more blessed than the immortal Gods, while I with greater art and skill in vengeance shall plunge you into new disasters. Pride great as mine does not stumble and fall at once. In a surrender so prompt you should beware the trap. You badly mistake faces for hearts if you believe a transformation so swift is sincere. What comes will show how changed I am!

[IV.vi]   *Enter* Seleucus.

CLEOPATRA.

Did you know, Seleucus, that I am avenged?

SELEUCUS.

Oh, poor princess!

CLEOPATRA.

Do you weep over her fate? Did you love her then?

SELEUCUS.

Enough to mourn her death.

CLEOPATRA.

You may continue as her faithful suitor. I have been avenged but not on her!

SELEUCUS.

Heaven help us! On whom then, madam?

CLEOPATRA.

On you, ingrate, who sought only to be her husband. On you, who adored her despite your mother's will; on you, who disdained to aid me in my wrath; on you, whose love rose up against my desire, opposed my vengeance, and laid waste to my pleasure.

SÉLEUCUS.

    De moi!

CLÉOPÂTRE.   De toi, perfide! Ignore, dissimule   1415
    Le mal que tu dois craindre et le feu qui te brûle,
    Et si pour l'ignorer tu crois t'en garantir,
    Du moins en l'apprenant commence à le sentir.
      Le trône était à toi par le droit de naissance,
    Rodogune avec lui tombait en ta puissance;   1420
    Tu devais l'épouser, tu devais être roi,
    Mais comme ce secret n'est connu que de moi,
    Je puis, comme je veux, tourner le droit d'aînesse,
    Et donne à ton rival ton sceptre et ta maîtresse.

SÉLEUCUS.

    A mon frère?

CLÉOPÂTRE.   C'est lui que j'ai nommé l'aîné.   1425

SÉLEUCUS.

    Vous ne m'affligez point de l'avoir couronné,
    Et par une raison qui vous est inconnue
    Mes propres sentiments vous avaient prévenue.
    Les biens que vous m'ôtez n'ont point d'attraits si doux
    Que mon cœur n'ait donnés à ce frère avant vous;   1430
    Et si vous bornez là toute votre vengeance,
    Vos désirs et les miens seront d'intelligence.

CLÉOPÂTRE.

    C'est ainsi qu'on déguise un violent dépit,
    C'est ainsi qu'une feinte au dehors l'assoupit,
    Et qu'on croit amuser de fausses patiences   1435
    Ceux dont en l'âme on craint les justes défiances.

SÉLEUCUS.

    Quoi! je conserverais quelque courroux secret!

CLÉOPÂTRE.

    Quoi! lâche, tu pourrais la perdre sans regret?
    Elle de qui les Dieux te donnaient l'hyménée,
    Elle dont tu plaignais la perte imaginée?   1440

SÉLEUCUS.

    Considérer sa perte avec compassion,
    Ce n'est pas aspirer à sa possession.

CLÉOPÂTRE.

    Que la mort la ravisse ou qu'un rival l'emporte,
    La douleur d'un amant est également forte,

SELEUCUS.

On me!

CLEOPATRA.

On you, deceitful child! Pretend to ignore the evils you should dread, the fire that burns you; and if you think that in ignorance you can save yourself from them, you shall at least by learning what they are begin to feel them.

The throne was yours by right of birth, and Rodogune with it was to be yours. You were to wed her; you were to be king. But since only I know the secret, I can do as I wish: turn aside the true right, and give your rival your scepter and your mistress.

SELEUCUS.

To my brother—

CLEOPATRA.

I have declared him the elder.

SELEUCUS.

You cause me no distress when you have crowned him, and for reasons you do not know my own feelings have forestalled you. What you take from me has no such great attraction that I do not gladly give it to my brother before you do so. If your vengeance is bounded by that, your desires accord with mine.

CLEOPATRA.

In that fashion one disguises a violent spite! In that fashion one feigns a calm exterior, meaning to delude with an appearance of patience those whose suspicions one rightly fears at heart.

SELEUCUS.

What do you mean? Do you suppose I am yet moved by hidden anger?

CLEOPATRA.

What do I mean? Are you a poltroon, that you could lose her without regret? The princess you were to wed by the Gods' decree? Whose false death you wept?

SELEUCUS.

One may weep her death without wanting to possess her.

CLEOPATRA.

Whether death steals her away or a rival bears her off, the pain of a lover is just as strong, and certain men who are

Et tel qui se console après l'instant fatal, 1445
Ne saurait voir son bien aux mains de son rival.
Piqué jusques au vif, il tâche à le reprendre,
Il fait de l'insensible, afin de mieux surprendre,
D'autant plus animé, que ce qu'il a perdu
Par rang ou par mérite à sa flamme était dû. 1450

SÉLEUCUS.

Peut-être, mais enfin par quel amour de mère
Pressez-vous tellement ma douleur contre un frère ?
Prenez-vous intérêt à la faire éclater ?

CLÉOPÂTRE.

J'en prends à la connaître, et la faire avorter,
J'en prends à conserver malgré toi mon ouvrage 1455
Des jaloux attentats de ta secrète rage.

SÉLEUCUS.

Je le veux croire ainsi, mais quel autre intérêt
Nous fait tous deux aînés quand et comme il vous plaît ?
Qui des deux vous doit croire, et par quelle justice
Faut-il que sur moi seul tombe tout le supplice, 1460
Et que du même amour dont nous sommes blessés
Il soit récompensé, quand vous m'en punissez ?

CLÉOPÂTRE.

Comme reine, à mon choix je fais justice ou grâce,
Et je m'étonne fort d'où vous vient cette audace,
D'où vient qu'un fils, vers moi noirci de trahison, 1465
Ose de mes faveurs me demander raison !

SÉLEUCUS.

Vous pardonnerez donc ces chaleurs indiscrètes.
Je ne suis point jaloux du bien que vous lui faites,
Et je vois quel amour vous avez pour tous deux,
Plus que vous ne pensez et plus que je ne veux. 1470
Le respect me défend d'en dire davantage.
  Je n'ai ni faute d'yeux ni faute de courage,
Madame, mais enfin n'espérez voir en moi
Qu'amitié pour mon frère, et zèle pour mon roi.
Adieu.

consoled after the fatal moment could not bear to see her in the hands of a rival. Pierced to the heart, they attempt to take her again; they show no feeling, to favor a surprise assault, and they are all the more angered that what they have lost was theirs by right of merit or station.

SELEUCUS.

That may be. But what kind of mother-love is it after all, which rouses me with such ardor against a brother? Where is your profit, if my pain breaks forth?

CLEOPATRA.

My profit is knowing it, in seeing to it that your plan miscarries! It is in preserving my work despite your efforts against the jealous violence of your secret rage.

SELEUCUS.

I would like to believe it so. But what other profit drives you to have one of us first-born, then the other, when and how you please? Which of us is to believe you, and where is the justice in the whole condemnation falling on me? And if this same love wounds us both, why is he rewarded while you punish me?

CLEOPATRA.

I am the queen! I condemn and I show favor as I please. And I wonder indeed whence comes this audacity, whence comes it that a son black with treason dares demand an explanation of my favors!

SELEUCUS.

You will pardon then the warmth of my indiscretion. I am not jealous of the grace you show him, and I see how you love us both, better than you know; better than I could wish. Respect forbids my saying more.

I lack neither eyes nor courage, madam, and in short, do not count on finding in me anything but affection for my brother and zeal for my king. Farewell.   *Exit* Seleucus.

[IV.vii]   Cléopâtre.

CLÉOPÂTRE.

De quel malheur suis-je encore capable ?   1475
Leur amour m'offensait, leur amitié m'accable,
Et contre mes fureurs je trouve en mes deux fils
Deux enfants révoltés, et deux rivaux unis.
Quoi ? sans émotion perdre trône et maîtresse !
Quel est ici ton charme, odieuse Princesse ?   1480
Et par quel privilège, allumant de tels feux,
Peux-tu n'en prendre qu'un, et m'ôter tous les deux ?
N'espère pas pourtant triompher de ma haine :
Pour régner sur deux cœurs, tu n'es pas encor reine.
Je sais bien qu'en l'état où tous deux je les voi,   1485
Il me les faut percer pour aller jusqu'à toi.
Mais n'importe, mes mains sur le père enhardies
Pour un bras refusé sauront prendre deux vies,
Leurs jours également sont pour moi dangereux :
J'ai commencé par lui, j'achèverai par eux.   1490
    Sors de mon cœur, nature, ou fais qu'ils m'obéissent :
Fais-les servir ma haine, ou consens qu'ils périssent.
Mais déjà l'un a vu que je les veux punir :
Souvent qui tarde trop se laisse prévenir.
Allons chercher le temps d'immoler mes victimes,   1495
Et de me rendre heureuse à force de grands crimes.

Fin du quatrième acte.

[IV.vii]   Cleopatra *alone*.

CLEOPATRA.

Are there still misfortunes in store for me? Their love was
an offense, their affection for one another overwhelms me.
I find in my two sons rebellious children and rivals united
against my rage. Can he indeed lose mistress and throne
unmoved? What spells have you wrought, detestable
woman! What prestige, what power excites such loves that
you can take but one and wrest them both from me? Do not
expect however to triumph over my hate. Two hearts under
your command do not make you queen already. I know
well that the state I find them in both forces me to pierce
them to come at you. But no matter, my hands hardened in
their father's blood will have the strength to take two lives
for the arm they have refused to lend me; their lives are just
as dangerous to me. I began with him, my achievement
shall end with them.

Out of my heart, all natural feeling, or bring obedience
to theirs! Make them serve my hatred or let them perish!
But this one sees already that I mean to punish them. He
who delays is often thwarted. Come, I must think when
to immolate my victims, how to win happiness as I heap
crime on crime.

                    End of the Fourth Act.

ACTE V

CLÉOPÂTRE.

Enfin, grâces aux Dieux, j'ai moins d'un ennemi:
La mort de Séleucus m'a vengée à demi.
Son ombre, en attendant Rodogune et son frère,
Peut déjà de ma part les promettre à son père.   1500
Ils le suivront de près, et j'ai tout préparé
Pour réunir bientôt ce que j'ai séparé.
O toi, qui n'attends plus que la cérémonie
Pour jeter à mes pieds ma rivale punie,
Et par qui deux amants vont d'un seul coup du sort   1505
Recevoir l'hyménée et le trône et la mort,
Poison, me sauras-tu rendre mon diadème?
Le fer m'a bien servie, en feras-tu de même?
Me seras-tu fidèle? Et toi, que me veux-tu,
Ridicule retour d'une sotte vertu,   1510
Tendresse dangereuse autant comme importune?
Je ne veux point pour fils l'époux de Rodogune,
Et ne vois plus en lui les restes de mon sang,
S'il m'arrache du trône et la met en mon rang.
    Reste du sang ingrat d'un époux infidèle,   1515
Héritier d'une flamme envers moi criminelle,
Aime mon ennemie, et péris comme lui.
Pour la faire tomber j'abattrai son appui;
Aussi bien sous mes pas c'est creuser un abîme,
Que retenir ma main sur la moitié du crime,   1520
Et te faisant mon roi, c'est trop me négliger,
Que te laisser sur moi père et frère à venger.
Qui se venge à demi court lui-même à sa peine:
Il faut ou condamner ou couronner sa haine.
Dût le peuple en fureur pour ses maîtres nouveaux   1525
De mon sang odieux arroser leurs tombeaux,
Dût le Parthe vengeur me trouver sans défense,
Dût le ciel égaler le supplice à l'offense,
Trône, à t'abandonner je ne puis consentir.

ACT V

[V.i]   Cleopatra *alone.*

CLEOPATRA.

At last, the Gods be thanked, I have one enemy the less.
With Seleucus dead my vengeance is half done. His spirit
that waits for Rodogune and his brother may now promise
the father they will be sent after, by me. They follow hard
upon, for all is ready, that those I have set apart may meet
again. Oh you, that wait but for the ceremony to cast
beneath my feet a stricken rival, to give with one mortal
blow this pair of lovers their wedding, their throne, and
their death, oh poison! Will you restore to me my crown?
I have been well served by steel! Can you do no less? Can
I not trust in you? But you, what do you ask of me again,
ridiculous, foolish virtue? Dangerous, meddling intruder!
No sons of mine shall be the husband of Rodogune! No
drop of my blood will I see in him, if he wrests me from
my throne and to that seat raises her!

And you, last ungrateful drop of the adulterer's blood,
you, heir to passions criminal towards me: love my
enemy, perish with her! For her destruction I would
demolish her every support; draw back before half my
crimes, and the abyss yawns beneath my feet! And if I make
you king over me I care too little for myself; too easily you
would avenge on me a father, a brother. Half a vengeance
is the road to self-destruction. My hatred I must condemn,
or it must be sovereign, though an enraged populace
water their rulers' new grave with my hated blood, though
vengeful Parthians find me helpless, though Heaven itself
mete out punishment equal to my crimes. Throne: never
by my will can I leave you! Rather be driven from you by

Par un coup de tonnerre il vaut mieux en sortir,   1530
Il vaut mieux mériter le sort le plus étrange:
Tombe sur moi le ciel, pourvu que je me venge!
J'en recevrai le coup d'un visage remis.
Il est doux de périr après ses ennemis,
Et de quelque rigueur que le destin me traite,   1535
Je perds moins à mourir qu'à vivre leur sujette.
      Mais voici Laonice; il faut dissimuler
Ce que le seul effet doit bientôt révéler.

[V.ii]   Cléopâtre *et* Laonice.

CLÉOPÂTRE.
Viennent-ils, nos amants?
LAONICE.   Ils approchent, Madame.
On lit dessus leur front l'allégresse de l'âme;   1540
L'amour s'y fait paraître avec la majesté,
Et suivant le vieil ordre en Syrie usité,
D'une grâce en tous deux toute auguste et royale
Ils viennent prendre ici la coupe nuptiale,
Pour s'en aller au temple au sortir du palais,   1545
Par les mains du grand prêtre être unis à jamais.
C'est là qu'il les attend pour bénir l'alliance,
Le peuple tout ravi par ses vœux le devance,
Et pour eux à grands cris demande aux immortels
Tout ce qu'on leur souhaite au pied de leurs autels,   1550
Impatient pour eux que la cérémonie
Ne commence bientôt, ne soit bientôt finie.
Les Parthes à la foule aux Syriens mêlés,
Tous nos vieux différends de leur âme exilés,
Font leur suite assez grosse, et d'une voix commune   1555
Bénissent à l'envi le Prince et Rodogune.
Mais je les vois déjà, Madame: c'est à vous
A commencer ici des spectacles si doux.

[V.iii]   Cléopâtre, Antiochus, Rodogune, Oronte, Laonice.
              Troupe de Parthes et de Syriens.

CLÉOPÂTRE.
Approchez, mes enfants, car l'amour maternelle,

the thunders of Jove, rather deserve the most monstrous fates, rather the heavens fall and crush me—so I have my revenge! Let the blows fall, I await them, serene. Sweet it is to die after the death of foes. Whatever my harsh fate may hold in store, dying is a lesser evil than living enslaved to them.

But here is Laonice; I must conceal what should be seen only in the results.

[V.ii]   Laonice *enters.*

CLEOPATRA.

Do our young lovers come?

LAONICE.

They do, madam. Heartfelt joy shines in their aspect, for Love appears in all his majesty, and in obedience to Syria's ancient law they come, with august and royal grace, to drink the wedding cup before going from palace to temple, where the high priest waits, to unite them forever and to bless their union. Their joys overflowing, the people come before his blessing with their own, and they call on the Gods immortal to grant the prayers said before the altar, impatient that the ceremonies soon begin, soon conclude. Parthians mingle with the Syrian crowd and swell the festive throng, banishing from their hearts the old quarrel, as in a single voice all give proof of devotion to the prince and to Rodogune. But here they come, madam. It is for you to begin this most joyful show.

[V.iii]
Enter Antiochus, Rodogune *and* Oronte *followed by Parthians and Syrians.*

CLEOPATRA.

Come near me, my children, for with a mother's heart and

Madame, dans mon cœur vous tient déjà pour telle,   1560
Et je crois que ce nom ne vous déplaira pas.

RODOGUNE.

Je le chérirai même au-delà du trépas ;
Il m'est trop doux, Madame, et tout l'heur que j'espère,
C'est de vous obéir et respecter en mère.

CLÉOPÂTRE.

Aimez-moi seulement, vous allez être rois,   1565
Et s'il faut du respect, c'est moi qui vous le dois.

ANTIOCHUS.

Ah ! si nous recevons la suprême puissance,
Ce n'est pas pour sortir de votre obéissance.
Vous régnerez ici quand nous y régnerons,
Et ce seront vos lois que nous y donnerons.   1570

CLÉOPÂTRE.

J'ose le croire ainsi, mais prenez votre place,
Il est temps d'avancer ce qu'il faut que je fasse.

Ici Antiochus *s'assied dans un fauteuil,* Rodogune *à sa gauche, en même rang, et* Cléopâtre *à sa droite, mais en rang inférieur, et qui marque quelque inégalité.* Oronte *s'assied aussi à la gauche de* Rodogune, *avec la même différence ; et* Cléopâtre, *cependant qu'ils prennent leurs places, parle à l'oreille de* Laonice, *qui s'en va quérir une coupe pleine de vin empoisonné. Après qu'elle est partie,* Cléopâtre *continue :*

Peuple qui m'écoutez, Parthes et Syriens,
Sujets du Roi son frère, ou qui fûtes les miens,
Voici de mes deux fils celui qu'un droit d'aînesse   1575
Élève dans le trône, et donne à la Princesse.
Je lui rends cet État que j'ai sauvé pour lui,
Je cesse de régner, il commence aujourd'hui.
Qu'on ne me traite plus ici de souveraine :
Voici votre Roi, peuple, et voilà votre Reine.   1580
Vivez pour les servir, respectez-les tous deux,
Aimez-les et mourez, s'il est besoin, pour eux.
    Oronte, vous voyez avec quelle franchise
Je leur rends ce pouvoir dont je me suis démise ;
Prêtez les yeux au reste, et voyez les effets   1585
Suivre de point en point les traités de la paix.

Laonice *revient avec une coupe à la main.*

love, madam, I count you already as one of my own; and I
dare believe the title is not displeasing to you.

RODOGUNE.

I shall cherish it beyond the grave. It is sweet indeed,
madam, and I wish for no other happiness than to obey and
respect in you a mother.

CLEOPATRA.

I ask only your love. You are to be king and queen, and
if respect is due, it is I who must render it to you.

ANTIOCHUS.

Ah, if we have reached the highest power, it is not to deny
obedience to you. Where we reign you shall reign there
too, and the laws we proclaim shall be your laws.

CLEOPATRA.

I dare believe it may be so! But take your places; it is time
I set about what I have to do.

Antiochus *takes an arm chair, with* Rodogune *on his left and at the same
level, and with* Cleopatra *on his right, but on a lower level, to indicate the
slight inferiority of rank.* Orontes *is at the same level on Rodogune's left.
Meanwhile* Cleopatra *whispers to* Laonice, *who goes to fetch a cup of
poisoned wine. After she has gone,* Cleopatra *continues:*

Parthians, Syrians! All who attend here, subjects of the
king, her brother, or all those subjects who once were
mine: this is my son, he that is raised to the throne by
prior right of birth, and this is he that is now wed to this
princess. To him I yield this state, that I have saved for
him. My reign is ended as his begins today. Look no more
to me as your sovereign. Here is your king, my people; and
here, your queen. Live for them, serve them, render to them
the respect that is their due. Give them your love and if
need be, your lives.

Orontes, you see how openly I give them the power I
strip from myself: bend your glance on what follows,
observe how point by point the treaty is executed.

Laonice *returns holding a cup.*

ORONTE.

Votre sincérité s'y fait assez paraître,
Madame, et j'en ferai récit au Roi mon maître.

CLÉOPÂTRE.

L'hymen est maintenant notre plus cher souci.
L'usage veut, mon fils, qu'on le commence ici;   1590
Recevez de ma main la coupe nuptiale,
Pour être après unis sous la foi conjugale.
Puisse-t-elle être un gage envers votre moitié,
De votre amour ensemble, et de mon amitié.

ANTIOCHUS [*prenant la coupe*].

Ciel! que ne dois-je point aux bontés d'une mère!   1595

CLÉOPÂTRE.

Le temps presse, et votre heur d'autant plus se diffère.

ANTIOCHUS [*à* Rodogune].

Madame, hâtons donc ces glorieux moments;
Voici l'heureux essai de nos contentements.
Mais si mon frère était le témoin de ma joie . . .

CLÉOPÂTRE.

C'est être trop cruel de vouloir qu'il la voie,   1600
Ce sont des déplaisirs qu'il fait bien d'épargner,
Et sa douleur secrète a droit de l'éloigner.

ANTIOCHUS.

Il m'avait assuré qu'il la verrait sans peine,
Mais n'importe, achevons.

[V.iv]

Cléopâtre, Antiochus, Rodogune, Oronte, Timagène, Laonice,
troupe.

TIMAGÈNE.   Ah! Seigneur.

CLÉOPÂTRE.   Timagène,
Quelle est votre insolence?

TIMAGÈNE.   Ah! Madame!

ANTIOCHUS [*rendant la coupe à* Laonice].   Parlez.   1605

TIMAGÈNE.

Souffrez pour un moment que mes sens rappelés . . .

ANTIOCHUS.

Qu'est-il donc arrivé?

ORONTES.

Your sincerity appears in all you do, madam, and my
master shall have in my report a full account.

CLEOPATRA.

The rites of Hymen are now our dearest concern. By
custom, my son, it must begin here. Take, from my hand,
this wedding cup and drink, before you are joined in
marriage. May it be a pledge to your betrothed of your
love and of my affection together!

ANTIOCHUS [*taking the cup*].

Just Heaven, what more can I owe to a mother's kindness?

CLEOPATRA.

Time presses and with every moment your happiness is the
more deferred.

ANTIOCHUS [*to* Rodogune].

Madam, let us hurry then these glorious moments; here is
the happy test of our joy. But if my brother were here to
witness my happiness—

CLEOPATRA.

It would be too cruel to insist that he see it, and he does
well to spare himself such hurt; his private sorrow gives
him every right to remain apart.

ANTIOCHUS.

He assured me he would look on without pain. But, no
matter, let us conclude—

[V.iv]   *Enter* Timagenes.

TIMAGENES.

Oh! My lord!

CLEOPATRA.

Timagenes, what insolence is this?

TIMAGENES.

Ah, madam!

ANTIOCHUS [*handing the cup to* Laonice].

Speak.

TIMAGENES.

A moment, I beseech you, to recover—

TIMAGÈNE.   Le Prince votre frère . . .

ANTIOCHUS.

Quoi ? se voudrait-il rendre à mon bonheur contraire ?

TIMAGÈNE.

L'ayant cherché longtemps afin de divertir
L'ennui que de sa perte il pouvait ressentir,   1610
Je l'ai trouvé, Seigneur, au bout de cette allée,
Où la clarté du ciel semble toujours voilée.
Sur un lit de gazon, de faiblesse étendu,
Il semblait déplorer ce qu'il avait perdu.
Son âme à ce penser paraissait attachée,   1615
Sa tête sur un bras languissamment penchée,
Immobile et rêveur, en malheureux amant . . .

ANTIOCHUS.

Enfin, que faisait-il ? achevez promptement.

TIMAGÈNE.

D'une profonde plaie en l'estomac ouverte,
Son sang à gros bouillons sur cette couche verte . . .   1620

CLÉOPÂTRE.

Il est mort ?

TIMAGÈNE.   Oui, Madame.

CLÉOPÂTRE.   Ah ! destins ennemis
Qui m'enviez le bien que je m'étais promis !
Voilà le coup fatal que je craignais dans l'âme,
Voilà le désespoir où l'a réduit sa flamme !
Pour vivre en vous perdant il avait trop d'amour,   1625
Madame, et de sa main il s'est privé du jour.

TIMAGÈNE [*à* Cléopâtre].

Madame, il a parlé, sa main est innocente.

CLÉOPÂTRE [*à* Timagène].

La tienne est donc coupable, et ta rage insolente
Par une lâcheté qu'on ne peut égaler,
L'ayant assassiné, le fait encor parler !   1630

ANTIOCHUS.

Timagène, souffrez la douleur d'une mère
Et les premiers soupçons d'une aveugle colère.
Comme ce coup fatal n'a point d'autres témoins,
J'en ferais autant qu'elle, à vous connaître moins.
Mais que vous a-t-il dit ? achevez, je vous prie.   1635

ANTIOCHUS.

But what has happened?

TIMAGENES.

The prince, your brother—

ANTIOCHUS.

What is it, would he destroy my happiness?

TIMAGENES.

For a long time I sought him, to see if I could distract his
mind from the pains his loss might have caused; and I
found him, my lord, at the end of that path where heaven's
light seems always veiled. Lying stretched out in his weakness on the grassy bed, he seemed to be mourning his loss,
his thoughts appeared fixed on that idea, for the head lay
languishing on his arm, motionless, lost in reverie, as we see
wretched lovers—

ANTIOCHUS.

But quickly, what was he doing? Come to the point!

TIMAGEMES.

I found him with his breast gashed open, and blood
spurting from the deep wound stained the green couch—

CLEOPATRA.

He is dead?

TIMAGENES.

Yes, madam.

CLEOPATRA.

Ah, cruel fates that envy me my promised joys! That is the
mortal stroke I feared in my heart, that is the despair of his
unhappy love. He loved you too much to live without you,
madam, and by his own hand cut short his days.

TIMAGENES [*to* Cleopatra].

Madam, he did speak, and his hand is innocent.

CLEOPATRA [*to* Timagenes].

Then yours is guilty! In your insolent rage, your monstrous
infamy, you put words in the mouth you murdered.

ANTIOCHUS.

Timagenes, be patient with a mother's grief, the hasty suspicions of blind wrath. As there are no other witnesses to
the mortal deed, my action might have been hers, but that
I know you too well. But what was it he said? I beg you,
come to the end.

TIMAGÈNE.

Surpris d'un tel spectacle, à l'instant je m'écrie,
Et soudain à mes cris, ce prince en soupirant
Avec assez de peine entr'ouvre un œil mourant,
Et ce reste égaré de lumière incertaine
Lui peignant son cher frère au lieu de Timagène,   1640
Rempli de votre idée, il m'adresse pour vous
Ces mots où l'amitié règne sur le courroux :
   «Une main qui nous fut bien chère
Venge ainsi le refus d'un coup trop inhumain.
   Régnez, et surtout, mon cher frère,   1645
   Gardez-vous de la même main.
C'est . . .» La Parque à ce mot lui coupe la parole,
Sa lumière s'éteint, et son âme s'envole ;
Et moi, tout effrayé d'un si tragique sort,
J'accours pour vous en faire un funeste rapport.   1650

ANTIOCHUS.

Rapport vraiment funeste, et sort vraiment tragique,
Qui va changer en pleurs l'allégresse publique.
O frère, plus aimé que la clarté du jour,
O rival, aussi cher que m'était mon amour,
Je te perds, et je trouve en ma douleur extrême   1655
Un malheur dans ta mort plus grand que ta mort même.
Oh ! de ses derniers mots fatale obscurité,
En quel gouffre d'horreurs m'as-tu précipité ?
Quand j'y pense chercher la main qui l'assassine,
Je m'impute à forfait tout ce que j'imagine.   1660
Mais aux marques enfin que tu m'en viens donner,
Fatale obscurité, qui dois-je en soupçonner ?
   «Une main qui nous fut bien chère!»
Madame, est-ce la vôtre, ou celle de ma mère ?
Vous vouliez toutes deux un coup trop inhumain ;   1665
Nous vous avons tous deux refusé notre main.
Qui de vous s'est vengée ? est-ce l'une, est-ce l'autre
Qui fait agir la sienne au refus de la nôtre ?
Est-ce vous qu'en coupable il me faut regarder ?
Est-ce vous désormais dont je me dois garder ?   1670

CLÉOPÂTRE.

Quoi ? vous me soupçonnez ?

RODOGUNE.   Quoi ? je vous suis suspecte ?

TIMAGENES.

Stunned by so dread a sight, I cried out at once, and suddenly, at the sound, the prince, sighing, painfully opened his dying eyes, and as the last bewildered flickering light pictured to him his beloved brother instead of Timagenes, filled with images of you, he spoke, mistaking me for you, these words, in which affection subdued wrath: "A hand once dear takes vengeance thus for refusing a too inhuman deed. Reign, and above all, dear brother beware this same hand. It was—" The Fates cut short his speech; the glimmer of life went out, and his soul took flight. And I, terrified by his tragic fate, hasten to you with the mournful tale.

ANTIOCHUS.

Truly a grievous tale! And truly a tragic fate that must turn our public joy to tears. Oh my brother, that I loved more than the light of day, oh rival, dear to me as my love; and I lose you but to glimpse in my bottomless grief a misfortune greater still than your death. Oh, fatal enigma of these last words! What is this horrible abyss where I sink? When I probe his words for the assassin's hand, my every thought is a crime, for in these dark and mortal hints, whose guilt must I see?

"A hand once dear . . . ." Is it yours, madam? Or is it my mother's? Both urged us to an inhuman deed; we both denied you our hand. Which of you has taken her revenge? Is it you—or you, whose hand took the place of ours, when we refused? Must I see in you the guilt? Must I be on guard with you, from this hour?

CLEOPATRA.

What! You suspect me?

RODOGUNE.

What! You have doubts of me?

ANTIOCHUS.

Je suis amant et fils, je vous aime et respecte.
Mais quoi que sur mon cœur puissent des noms si doux,
A ces marques enfin je ne connais que vous.
As-tu bien entendu? dis-tu vrai, Timagène? 1675

TIMAGÈNE.

Avant qu'en soupçonner la Princesse ou la Reine,
Je mourrais mille fois, mais enfin mon récit
Contient, sans rien de plus, ce que le Prince a dit.

ANTIOCHUS.

D'un et d'autre côté l'action est si noire,
Que n'en pouvant douter, je n'ose encor la croire. 1680
O quiconque des deux avez versé son sang,
Ne vous préparez plus à me percer le flanc!
Nous avons mal servi vos haines mutuelles,
Aux jours l'une de l'autre également cruelles.
Mais si j'ai refusé ce détestable emploi, 1685
Je veux bien vous servir toutes deux contre moi:
Qui que vous soyez donc, recevez une vie
Que déjà vos fureurs m'ont à demi ravie.

[*Il tire son épée et veut se tuer.*]

RODOGUNE.

Ah! Seigneur, arrêtez.

TIMAGÈNE.   Seigneur, que faites-vous?

ANTIOCHUS.

Je sers ou l'une ou l'autre, et je préviens ses coups. 1690

CLÉOPÂTRE.

Vivez, régnez heureux.

ANTIOCHUS.   Otez-moi donc de doute,
Et montrez-moi la main qu'il faut que je redoute,
Qui pour m'assassiner ose me secourir,
Et me sauve de moi pour me faire périr.
Puis-je vivre et traîner cette gêne éternelle, 1695
Confondre l'innocente avec la criminelle,
Vivre, et ne pouvoir plus vous voir sans m'alarmer,
Vous craindre toutes deux, toutes deux vous aimer?
Vivre avec ce tourment, c'est mourir à toute heure.

ANTIOCHUS.

> I am your betrothed; I am your son. I love and I respect
> you. Despite the tender sovereignty such words have in my
> soul, by these signs I recognize none but you. Did you
> hear him well, Timagenes? Is what you say true?

TIMAGENES.

> I will die a thousand deaths before I suspect the princess or
> my queen, but still, my story contains all and no more than
> what the prince did say.

ANTIOCHUS.

> From either one it is a deed so monstrous that though I
> cannot doubt, I dare not believe.
>
> Oh, whoever has shed his blood, you need prepare no
> more to pierce my heart! We served but ill your mutual
> hates, when you cruelly sought each other's death. But,
> though I refused that heinous command, you both may use
> me against myself! Whoever you are, take this life your
> furies have half destroyed!

> [*He draws his sword and tries to stab himself.*]

RODOGUNE.

> Stop, my lord, no!

TIMAGENES.

> My lord, what are you doing?

ANTIOCHUS.

> I lend my hand to one or to the other; I forestall her attack.

CLEOPATRA.

> Live, reign, and be happy!

ANTIOCHUS.

> Then remove my doubt! Show me the hand I ought to fear,
> which dares preserve me to murder me, stays my hand to
> destroy me with her own! Can I live, sinking under the
> endless torment, mistaking the innocent and the criminal;
> live, and never look on you but with alarm? Can I live
> fearing you both, loving you both. Such living torment is

Tirez-moi de ce trouble, ou souffrez que je meure,   1700
Et que mon déplaisir, par un coup généreux,
Épargne un parricide à l'une de vous deux.

CLÉOPÂTRE.

Puisque le même jour que ma main vous couronne
Je perds un de mes fils, et l'autre me soupçonne,
Qu'au milieu de mes pleurs, qu'il devrait essuyer,   1705
Son peu d'amour me force à me justifier,
Si vous n'en pouvez mieux consoler une mère,
Qu'en la traitant d'égale avec une étrangère,
Je vous dirai, Seigneur (car ce n'est plus à moi
A nommer autrement et mon juge et mon Roi),   1710
Que vous voyez l'effet de cette vieille haine
Qu'en dépit de la paix me garde l'inhumaine,
Qu'en son cœur du passé soutient le souvenir,
Et que j'avais raison de vouloir prévenir.
Elle a soif de mon sang, elle a voulu l'épandre.   1715
J'ai prévu d'assez loin ce que j'en viens d'apprendre,
Mais je vous ai laissé désarmer mon courroux.

A Rodogune.

Sur la foi de ses pleurs je n'ai rien craint de vous,
Madame, mais, ô Dieux! quelle rage est la vôtre!
Quand je vous donne un fils, vous assassinez l'autre,   1720
Et m'enviez soudain l'unique et faible appui
Qu'une mère opprimée eût pu trouver en lui!
Quand vous m'accablerez, où sera mon refuge?
Si je m'en plains au Roi, vous possédez mon juge,
Et s'il m'ose écouter, peut-être, hélas! en vain   1725
Il voudra se garder de cette même main.
Enfin je suis leur mère, et vous leur ennemie,
J'ai recherché leur gloire, et vous leur infamie,
Et si je n'eusse aimé ces fils que vous m'ôtez,
Votre abord en ces lieux les eût déshérités.   1730
C'est à lui maintenant, en cette concurrence,
A régler ses soupçons sur cette différence,
A voir de qui des deux il doit se défier,
Si vous n'avez un charme à vous justifier.

death at every hour. Let me escape this trouble or let me die; let my misery with one brave thrust spare one of you the parricidal crime.

CLEOPATRA.

Since on the very day my hand has crowned you I lose one of my sons and the other suspects me; since on the day my tears flow, that he should wipe away, his feeble love calls me to defend myself; if you can console your mother in no better way than to treat her as you do a foreign woman, I shall say to you, sire, for I may not otherwise address my judge and my king, that you see a result of the old hatred this inhuman creature has kept against me, in spite of the treaty, a hatred past memories keep strong in her heart, that I rightly wanted to forestall. She thirsts for my blood; she wanted to spill it. I foresaw, and long ago, what has just been proved to me, but I let you disarm my wrath.

To Rodogune.

I swear by the tears of my son, I feared nothing from you, madam, but oh! Heavens, how wild is your rage? I give you one son—and you murder the other. You were envious, at once, of the feeble support an oppressed mother might have found only in him. When you cast me down, where is my refuge? If I complain to my king, you own my judge! And if he should dare listen, perhaps, alas, he would be helpless before that very hand. When all is said, I am their mother, you their enemy. I have worked for their glory, you for their shame! And had I not loved the sons you steal from me, you, coming to their land, would have left them destitute. He may in this struggle govern his suspicions by that difference. He can see whom he should distrust, unless your sorcerer's arts can prove you innocent.

RODOGUNE [*à* Cléopâtre].

Je me défendrai mal. L'innocence étonnée 1735
Ne peut s'imaginer qu'elle soit soupçonnée,
Et n'ayant rien prévu d'un attentat si grand,
Qui l'en veut accuser, sans peine la surprend.
    Je ne m'étonne point de voir que votre haine
Pour me faire coupable a quitté Timagène: 1740
Au moindre jour ouvert de tout jeter sur moi,
Son récit s'est trouvé digne de votre foi.
Vous l'accusiez pourtant, quand votre âme alarmée
Craignait qu'en expirant ce fils vous eût nommée;
Mais de ses derniers mots voyant le sens douteux 1745
Vous avez pris soudain le crime entre nous deux.
Certes, si vous voulez passer pour véritable
Que l'une de nous deux de sa mort soit coupable,
Je veux bien par respect ne vous imputer rien;
Mais votre bras au crime est plus fait que le mien, 1750
Et qui sur un époux fit son apprentissage
A bien pu sur un fils achever son ouvrage.
Je ne dénierai point, puisque vous les savez,
De justes sentiments dans mon âme élevés:
Vous demandiez mon sang, j'ai demandé le vôtre. 1755
Le Roi sait quels motifs ont poussé l'une et l'autre;
Comme par sa prudence il a tout adouci,
Il vous connaît peut-être, et me connaît aussi.

A Antiochus.

Seigneur, c'est un moyen de vous être bien chère
Que pour don nuptial vous immoler un frère. 1760
On fait plus, on m'impute un coup si plein d'horreur,
Pour me faire un passage à vous percer le cœur.

A Cléopâtre.

Où fuirais-je de vous après tant de furie,
Madame, et que ferait toute votre Syrie,
Où, seule et sans appui contre mes attentats, 1765
Je verrais . . . ? Mais, Seigneur, vous ne m'écoutez pas.

ANTIOCHUS.

Non, je n'écoute rien, et dans la mort d'un frère
Je ne veux point juger entre vous et ma mère.

RODOGUNE [*to* Cleopatra].

My defense is weak indeed. Bewildered innocence cannot imagine herself suspected. Unable to foresee crimes so heinous, the accusation catches her at once off guard.

I am not surprised at all that your hate flew from Timagenes to accuse me. At the smallest chance to throw all the guilt on me, suddenly his tale merits your belief. Yet you were accusing him, when in fear and alarm that your son had named you as he died. But now, with the obscurity of his last words, you instantly agree the crime lies between the two of us. To be sure, if you insist that one of us is proved guilty without doubt, in respect, I intend to accuse you of nothing. But your hand is more used to crime than mine; a woman whose apprentice work was a husband may well pass as master on her son. I shall not deny, since you know of them, the feelings justly stirred in my soul. You asked for my blood, I for yours. The king knows by what motives both were moved. As in his great prudence he brought appeasement in everything, he knows you doubtless, and me as well.

To Antiochus.

My lord, it is a great show of love, to sacrifice your brother as a wedding gift. More than that, the horrible deed is thrown on me, to make of me a path by which to pierce your heart.

To Cleopatra.

Where should I escape your great fury, madam, and what would all your Syria do, where homeless, helpless against your attack, I could find—? But, sire, you do not hear me!

ANTIOCHUS.

No, I hear nothing. I will not judge between you and my mother on the death of Seleucus. Murder your son. Slay

Assassinez un fils, massacrez un époux,
Je ne veux me garder ni d'elle, ni de vous.   1770
   Suivons aveuglément ma triste destinée;
Pour m'exposer à tout achevons l'hyménée.
Cher frère, c'est pour moi le chemin du trépas;
La main qui t'a percé ne m'épargnera pas;
Je cherche à te rejoindre, et non à m'en défendre,   1775
Et lui veux bien donner tout lieu de me surprendre,
Heureux, si sa fureur qui me prive de toi
Se fait bientôt connaître en achevant sur moi.
Et si du ciel trop lent à la réduire en poudre
Son crime redoublé peut arracher la foudre!   1780
Donnez-moi . . .

RODOGUNE [*l'empêchant de prendre la coupe*].
              Quoi? Seigneur.

ANTIOCHUS.   Vous m'arrêtez en vain,
Donnez.

RODOGUNE.   Ah! gardez-vous de l'une et l'autre main.
Cette coupe est suspecte, elle vient de la Reine.
Craignez de toutes deux quelque secrète haine.

CLÉOPÂTRE.
Qui m'épargnait tantôt ose enfin m'accuser!   1785

RODOGUNE.
De toutes deux, Madame, il doit tout refuser.
Je n'accuse personne, et vous tiens innocente:
Mais il en faut sur l'heure une preuve évidente.
Je veux bien à mon tour subir les mêmes lois,
On ne peut craindre trop pour le salut des rois.   1790
Donnez donc cette preuve, et pour toute réplique,
Faites faire un essai par quelque domestique.

CLÉOPÂTRE [*prenant la coupe*].
Je le ferai moi-même. Eh bien! redoutez-vous
Quelque sinistre effet encor de mon courroux?
J'ai souffert cet outrage avecque patience.   1795

ANTIOCHUS [*prenant la coupe des mains de* Cléopâtre, *après qu'elle a bu*].
Pardonnez-lui, Madame, un peu de défiance.
Comme vous l'accusez, elle fait son effort
A rejeter sur vous l'horreur de cette mort,
Et soit amour pour moi, soit adresse pour elle,
Ce soin la fait paraître un peu moins criminelle.   1800

your husband. I guard myself neither from you nor from
her.

We must blindly work out my wretched fate. To throw
off all armor, let the wedding go on. Dear brother, there
lies for me the road to death. The hand that stabbed you
will not long spare me. I long to join you, not to put up
defenses; she will have every chance to catch me off guard,
and I shall be happy when the rage that deprived me of
you is revealed as she finishes her work on me, happy if
Heaven that too slowly crushes her to dust, would loose on
her redoubled crimes its thunder! Give that to me—

RODOGUNE [*prevents him from taking the cup*].

Sire, what—?

ANTIOCHUS.

It is useless to interfere. Give it to me!

RODOGUNE.

Ah, guard against both of us! That cup is suspect: it comes
from the queen. Beware the hate concealed on either side!

CLEOPATRA.

She who spared me just now dares accuse me at last!

RODOGUNE.

He must refuse, madam, what comes from you or me. I
accuse no one. I hold you guiltless, but we must have solid
proof at once. I willingly undergo the test. We cannot fear
too much for the safety of kings. Let us then have proof,
rather than words. Have some servant test the cup.

CLEOPATRA [*takes the cup*].

I shall test it myself. (*She drinks.*) Well! Do you still
fear some sinister effect of my wrath? I have suffered this
outrage patiently enough!

ANTIOCHUS [*takes the cup from Cleopatra after she has drunk*].

Pardon her, madam, if she cannot trust. As you accuse her,
she must throw back on you the horror of that death. Be it
love for me or shrewd defense of herself, such care lessens
somewhat in her the appearance of criminal guilt. As for

Pour moi, qui ne vois rien, dans le trouble où je suis,
Qu'un gouffre de malheurs, qu'un abîme d'ennuis,
Attendant qu'en plein jour ces vérités paraissent,
J'en laisse la vengeance aux Dieux qui les connaissent,
Et vais sans plus tarder . . .

RODOGUNE.   Seigneur, voyez ses yeux   1805
Déjà tous égarés, troubles et furieux,
Cette affreuse sueur qui court sur son visage,
Cette gorge qui s'enfle. Ah, bons Dieux, quelle rage!
Pour vous perdre après elle, elle a voulu périr.

ANTIOCHUS [*rendant la coupe à* Laonice *ou à quelque autre*].
N'importe, elle est ma mère, il faut la secourir.   1810

CLÉOPÂTRE.
Va, tu me veux en vain rappeler à la vie.
Ma haine est trop fidèle, et m'a trop bien servie:
Elle a paru trop tôt pour te perdre avec moi,
C'est le seul déplaisir qu'en mourant je reçoi.
Mais j'ai cette douceur dedans cette disgrâce   1815
De ne voir point régner ma rivale en ma place.
   Règne: de crime en crime enfin te voilà roi:
Je t'ai défait d'un père, et d'un frère, et de moi.
Puisse le ciel tous deux vous prendre pour victimes,
Et laisser choir sur vous les peines de mes crimes!   1820
Puissiez-vous ne trouver dedans votre union
Qu'horreur, que jalousie, et que confusion!
Et pour vous souhaiter tous les malheurs ensemble,
Puisse naître de vous un fils qui me ressemble.

ANTIOCHUS.
Ah! vivez pour changer cette haine en amour!   1825

CLÉOPÂTRE.
Je maudirais les Dieux s'ils me rendaient le jour.
Qu'on m'emporte d'ici. Je me meurs, Laonice;
Si tu veux m'obliger par un dernier service,
Après les vains efforts de mes inimitiés,
Sauve-moi de l'affront de tomber à leurs pieds.   1830

Elle s'en va, et Laonice *lui aide à marcher.*

ORONTE.
Dans les justes rigueurs d'un sort si déplorable,
Seigneur, le juste ciel vous est bien favorable.

me, blind in my confusion, I see nothing but a pit of misfortune, an abyss of misery; until in the light of day the
truth shines forth, vengeance I leave to all-knowing Gods,
and so, to delay no more, I shall—

RODOGUNE.

Sire, look! Her eyes roll wild, furious, glazed! Ghastly
sweat runs down her face, and look! How her throat swells!
Oh Gods above! She is mad! To drag you after, she wanted
to die!

ANTIOCHUS [*gives the cup to* Laonice *or to another*].

No matter: she is my mother, she must be helped.

CLEOPATRA.

Get away, it is useless. I shall not return to this life. My
hate is too loyal; it serves me too well. It showed too soon
and I could not destroy you with myself. In my dying there
is but that great displeasure. But it is sweet in my misfortune not to see my rival on my throne.

Begin your reign; from crime to crime you are king at
last. I have rid you of father, brother, and of me. May the
Heavens now mark you as the next victims, let fall on you
the punishment of all my crimes! Together in marriage,
may you find nothing but horror, jealousy, all confusion!
To wish you all misfortunes in one: may you beget a son
like me!

ANTIOCHUS.

Oh live, and change your hate to love!

CLEOPATRA.

I would curse the Gods who would give me life again.
Take me from this place. I am dying, Laonice. Oblige me,
it is your last service. My attacks have failed; spare me the
shame of falling at my enemies' feet. Laonice *helps her off.*

ORONTES.

Sire, Heaven's stern justice that appears in this deplorable
destiny is favorable to you indeed. At the edge of disaster,

Il vous a préservé, sur le point de périr,
Du danger le plus grand que vous pussiez courir,
Et par un digne effet de ses faveurs puissantes, 1835
La coupable est punie et vos mains innocentes.

ANTIOCHUS.

Oronte, je ne sais, dans son funeste sort,
Qui m'afflige le plus, ou sa vie, ou sa mort.
L'une et l'autre a pour moi des malheurs sans exemple.
Plaignez mon infortune. Et vous, allez au temple 1840
Y changer l'allégresse en un deuil sans pareil,
La pompe nuptiale en funèbre appareil,
Et nous verrons après, par d'autres sacrifices,
Si les Dieux voudront être à nos vœux plus propices.

FIN

it has preserved you from the greatest dangers you could incur. By the highest effects of its irresistible grace the guilty one is punished, and your hands are innocent.

ANTIOCHUS.

Orontes, I cannot tell what in that dreadful existence afflicts me more, her life or her death. Both have been for me disasters without equal. Pity my misfortunes. And you [*addressing the Syrians*], go to the temple. Let deepest mourning take the place of joy; let nuptial celebrations give way to funeral rites. We shall see, after other sacrifices, whether the Gods will be more propitious to our hopes.

FINIS

NOTES

[Acteurs]

1. *Cléopâtre*] By coincidence the heroines' names connote motive and character. Cleopatra, "of glorious paternity," evokes ambition; Rhodogune, a literal Greek translation of the Old Iranian **wr̥da-gaunā*, "rosy complexion," means therefore Rose (girl) and by almost universal poetic tradition symbolizes love. On conceptual orientation revealed in the use of names in Corneille see Robert J. Nelson, *Corneille, His Heroes and Their Worlds* (Philadelphia, 1963), p. 24, quoting L. Harvey's analysis of this feature of *La Suivante* in *Symposium* 13(1957): 293.

1. *Nicanor*] instead of Demetrius, for euphony. Josephus is the authority for this misreading of Nicator, Demetrius' actual surname (*Jew. Ant.* 13.12). The historical Nicanor was a general sent by Demetrius I Soter against Judaea (1 Maccabees 7. 26–49).

6. *Timagène*] It may well be by design that a pedagogue who requests the full account of Nicanor's captivity and death bears the name of the earliest historian known to be a direct source for extant knowledge of the Seleucids. See Appendix.

9. *Séleucie*] on the coast twelve miles from Antioch, the old capital of Syria.

9. *palais royal*] See Corneille, *Discours des trois unités:* strict unity of place is not possible in *Rodogune*. The first and third acts are set in Rodogune's antechamber, the second in the queen's apartments, the fourth in some small room on neutral ground, and the last in a throne room or hall.

[*Rodogune*]

18. *gêner*] here in the obsolescent meaning of physical torture.

19. *esclave*] Compare Nicanor's captivity in Parthia. By this detail Laonice indicates the bitterness of the rivalry before the cause is revealed.

27. *adroite fuite*] the legendary tactic of Parthian cavalry. See note below, line 1050 (III.v).

30. *Tryphon*] the name, apparently signifying "arrogance," adopted by a former minister of Cleopatra's first husband, Alexander Balas. Tryphon attempted to rule through the infant son of Alexander and Cleopatra. He was accused of then killing his princely hostage to set himself up as Tryphon I. See Josephus (*Jew. Ant.* 34).

38. *son frère*] in fact her uncle, Ptolemy VII. Seleucus and Antiochus would have found little safety in Memphis, and they were reared in Athens.

48. *femme*] The historical reason was that Cleopatra was a foreigner. Corneille suppresses that circumstance perhaps to avoid inferences that his protagonist was a commentary on Anne of Austria.

51. *son frère*] Nicanor's brother Antiochus VII Sidetes.

75. *fortune*] the general circumstances of one's life.

77. *secret*] with "doubt," "mask," "disguise," etc., a structural and lexical motif of the play. On the verisimilitude of Cleopatra's secret, see Introduction.

84. *rompre le coup*] prevent, stop a blow. Present usage: deaden the force of a blow.

108. *amitié*] affection, love in any relationship.

115. *fatal*] fated, fateful; sometimes (as here) ruinous.

121. *charmant*] casting a magic spell.

136. *l'Asie*] Here the translation follows the 1647 variant.

152. *vertu*] forcefulness, strength of character.

154. *lâche*] In courtly love ethos, Venus as well as Mars has her heroes, cowards, villains.

155. *courage*] feeling, passion.

167. *conseil*] decision.

221. *fortune*] The word is capitalized in some early editions, for example 1682, suggesting that the goddess is meant.

228. *plus cruelle*] This improbable rumor (see Appendix) renders the ignoble incest venial. But compare *Sophonisbe*, after the Fronde. Corneille's different handling of the dilemma is a measure of the evolution of morals.

266. *eût*] expresses the modality of possibility after negation.

295. *confidence*] a secret shared with a trusted friend.

299. *menace*] The dismal prophecy in Renaissance tragedy is usually confirmed by subsequent events.

354. *feux*] desires, love. By 1644 such metaphors retained little icasticity.

367. *chimère*] A passion inexplicable at first to Rodogune is not ultimately so either to herself or to the spectator. The "same blood, same worth" of the brothers are gifts of Nature and Fortune and therefore exterior to individual character. Lovers in Corneille must usually be endowed with such gifts, but great worth alone does not inspire passion. The *je ne sais quoi* of line 362 refers to a phenomenon experienced by all lovers who go on to form permanent mutual bonds: the intuitive recognition of a unique merit or value that each represents for the other, the sense that love, though mysterious in its ways, tends to unite those who belong together. In some modern commentary Seleucus is said to be superior to Antiochus, and Rodogune's "inexplicable" preference is taken to be evidence of the basic amorality of the play. *Chimère* is then understood in its strict meaning of an impossible, absurd phenomenon, and it is presumed to refer to the passion itself. But for Corneille's public, doubtless Rodogune's choice was neither irrational nor amoral. The two princes are intended to be admirable in contrasting ways, and it is on the younger that Corneille bestowed the *mérites* specifically lovable in a suitor. To arouse princesses like Rodogune to passion, the kind of heroism that may, and in the case of Seleucus does, lead to renunciation

will not be enough. One must be heroic as a lover and as a prince. Compare (in *Polyeucte*) Pauline's quick transference of passion from the noble pagan Sévère to her husband when the latter exhibits Roman fortitude and magnanimity as well as the more Christian virtues she had already seen. The occurrence is meant to symbolize the action of divine grace, but it is sound psychology too. The *chimère*, in the case of Rodogune, is the miracle, as it seems to her, that she can sense Antiochus' potential merits as the lover she needs for both subjective and objective reasons before she can have seen it in his actions. But intuition of this kind did not in the era of Descartes seem irrational in the modern sense of the term, that is, without real, knowable causes that, when known, make phenomena intelligible.

398. *fantômes*] the insubstantial promises made by Cleopatra for *raison d'état*.

413. *gloire*] acquired in proportion to the extraordinary quality of a life, whether in the accomplishment of good or evil.

422. *à la main*] concludes a syllepsis. *Ta vengeance* and *mon sceptre* require that *mettre à la main* have a literal and a metaphorical meaning simultaneously.

428. *pompeux*] festive. Compare with *style pompeux*, cultivated in Corneille's era: sublime and ceremonial.

468. *eût*] optative. Compare with line 266 (I.iv).

476. *Délices*] introduces erotic images that show Cleopatra paradoxically to be a figure of ambition.

494. *et combattre pour moi*] elliptical. Read *pour qu'il combatte pour moi*.

510. *à son frère*] *Son* refers to Rodogune. Syntactical obscurity of this kind will be strongly criticized for the next three centuries.

585. *amour*] often feminine in poetry before 1700.

619. *la même infamie*] that is, *l'infamie même*.

633. *attenté*] connotes violence, crime.

672. *Point d'aîné*] See Jacques Scherer, ed., *Rodogune* (Paris, 1946), pp. 52–53, for Voltaire's comment on this tirade.

679. *Mégère*] Since this is also a common noun in French, it is less erudite than the English Megaera. Hence my translation.

701. *rien*] a positive here.

719. *stupide*] insensible.

724. *sort*] *Sort* in early editions. The initial capital, and the following comma, which marks a non-restrictive clause, imply the reading, "I blame an impersonal fate, that is, chance." For a discussion of metaphysical ideas in *Rodogune*, see Judd D. Hubert, "The Conflict between Chance and Morality in *Rodogune*," *Modern Language Notes* 74 (1959): 234–39.

798. *généreux*] courageous, noble. See Nelson (above, n. 1), p. 21 for an explication of the word and discussions of the concept with reference to critiques of Herland, Bénichou, Nadal, et al.

826. *pussions*] Most modern editors have altered this to *puissions*.

Compare *pûssions* in the 1682 edition. This edition follows Marty-Laveaux and modernizes only to the extent of removing the circumflex accent.

854. *lui*] refers to *amour* (line 851). The topos (subjection of love by will) and figure (antimetabole) are typically Cornelian. Note that *amour* is usually masculine in this play.

872. *on*] refers to Phraates and his troops.

890. *le jour*] is the stem of a syllepsis.

922. *sujet*] part of an untranslatable play on words.

1050. *en Parthe*] alludes to the tactic of mounted Parthian bowmen, who were adept at loosing their arrows backwards while in tactical retreat at full gallop. The preciosity of the metaphor is no doubt exaggerated, but it may not be entirely inappropriate to the following debate in which the casuistries of *raison d'état* and of courtly love are symmetrically opposed.

1130. *La nature, et l'amour*] The comma is from the 1682 edition. It distinguishes between those to whom appeals to maternal instinct and to love will be addressed.

1154. *époux*] is already obsolete in this meaning. See Scherer, *Rodogune* (above, n. 672), p. 75, note.

1158. *son cœur*] This and the following enthymeme recall *emblemata* of counter-Reformation literature, where hearts are portrayed with eyes, knees (the genuflecting heart), wings, uplifted arms, and the like. Note also the anaphora of lines 1159–61, the paronymy of lines 1162–64, and especially the linear displacement of morphemes of *aimer*. Corneille's return to stylistic mannerisms of *Clitandre* and *Le Cid* may account in part for the extremes of favor and disfavor to which *Rodogune* has been subjected.

1183. *Satisfaites vous-même*] The rest of the scene is patterned on *Le Cid*, III.iv.

1253. *Et prête-lui*] *Lui* refers to *nature*.

1268. *périr*] Cleopatra's plans miscarry because her conviction on this point is so strong that she counts on ambition to drive her sons and Rodogune irresistibly, as it does her.

1357. *l'aîné*] Regarding the order of birth Cleopatra has lost credibility. Note that the secret is never explicitly revealed in the play.

1370. *aimé*] Cleopatra too recognizes the effect of the sympathy described by Rodogune in Act I.

1415. *De toi*] The singular form here indicates contempt.

1436. *défiances*] The argument echoes lines 312–27 (I.v).

1485. *voi*] (instead of *vois*) is an orthography for visual rhyme.

1491. *nature*] If, as Nelson and others believe, this line suggests a conflict of maternal love and ambition, it is too late to soften the granitic impression left by the queen. Possibly no more should be sought here than a realistic detail (purely physical revulsion from a deed she must recognize to be murder and not an act of war or statecraft) or an echo of *Medea*. The two possibilities are not mutually exclusive.

1619. *estomac*] instead of *poitrine* is required by linguistic decorum.

1734. *charme*] echoes line 1480 (IV.vii).

1751. *Et qui*] The following couplet echoes line 1490 (IV.vii).

1806. *tous*] Modern usage would require *tout*.

1816. *en ma place*] The following lines were deleted by Corneille after 1660:

> Je n'aimais que le trône, et de son droit douteux
> J'espérais faire un don fatal à tous les deux,
> Détruire l'un par l'autre et régner en Syrie
> Plutôt par vos fureurs que par ma barbarie.
> Ton frère, avecque toi trop fortement uni,
> Ne m'a point écoutée et je l'en ai puni.
> J'ai cru par ce poison en faire autant du reste.
> Mais sa force, trop prompte, à moi seule est funeste.

(I loved only the throne, and I hoped to make of the uncertain prior right a gift fatal to you both, to destroy one through the other, and to reign in Syria thanks rather to your furious rage than by my savagery. Your brother was too closely bound to you; he would not listen to me, and I punished him for that. I thought with this poison to do as much to the rest of you, but it has struck with all its power too soon and is deadly for me alone.)

1820. *sur vous les peines*] a reversal of lines 579–82 (II.iii).

1824. *ressemble*] Compare Seneca's *liberos* . . . *similesque matri* (*Medea*, lines 24–25). But it may have been the death of Cleopatra IV that inspired Corneille to paraphrase Seneca in the context.

APPENDIX

A Note on the Use of Historical Sources in *Rodogune* and a Chronology of the Kings of Syria from 150 to 65 B.C.

Although the early complete accounts of the reigns of Demetrius II Nicator and his sons compiled by Greek historians of the first and second centuries before Christ did not survive, the substance was preserved temporarily by Gnaeus Pompeius Trogus, called the epitomator of Timagenes, his principal source, in *Historiae philippicae et totius mundi origines et terrae situs*. Most of this work perished also and is known primarily through the *Epitoma Historiarum Philippicarum Pompei Trogi* by Justin. Parts of the history of Demetrius had been given also by Flavius Josephus in *Jewish Antiquities* and by Appian of Alexandria, in his *Roman History* (XI.67–69). The first writes copiously of the events leading to Demetrius' death, but he says nothing of his sons, whose conflicts with Cleopatra and with each other are of no importance to his subject. Appian, insofar as Corneille's characters are concerned, might well be called the epitomator of Justin, for he omits much and romanticizes the rest. Other ancient writers (Livy, 1 Maccabees, Eusebius, Strabo et al.) add little to knowledge of the events on which *Rodogune* is based. In sum, for the play proper there are but two sources of any importance, Appian and Justin. To enable the reader to appraise the unacknowledged debt to the latter, essential passages from the *Universal History* are given below in a literal translation as part of a chronology compiled principally from *The House of Seleucus* (London, 1902; Barnes and Noble reprint, 1966) by Edwyn R. Bevan and the *Histoire des Séleucides*, 2 vols. (Paris, 1913–14) by A. Bouché-Leclercq. Since Corneille borrowed many details indirectly, by inference or by transference from one personage or episode to another, quotations of special importance from Justin are italicized. My comments appear in brackets.

150 B.C.   *The Reign of Alexander I Balas*

Alexander, who claimed the throne through his putative father, Antiochus IV, with an army of Syrian rebels and the assistance of Rome and Egypt defeated the unpopular Demetrius I. The latter died in battle and the succession of the rightful heir, Demetrius (II), Corneille's Nicanor, was blocked.

148 B.C.

The usurper proved weak, cruel, and mercenary. The new reign was more unpopular than the preceding had been, and the Syrians were ready to welcome another claimant. Ptolemy VI of Egypt seized this opportunity to control Syria through Alexander by bringing him an army and his daughter to wife, the fourteen-year-old Cleopatra, surnamed Thea. A son, Antiochus (VI), was born. The eleven-year-old Demetrius (II) was given the surname Nicator (Nicanor in Josephus, but this variant was probably a scribal error) and was brought to Syria by a band of Cretan adventurers. Having gained the support of a majority of the Syrian Greeks, Demetrius ousted Alexander. Ptolemy then transferred to the victor his support and Cleopatra as well, handing her over to Demetrius "as if she were a piece of furniture" (Bevan). She was at least three years older than her new husband and detested him from the start.

145 B.C.   *The first reign of Demetrius II*

Ptolemy was killed in a final battle against Alexander's dwindling forces and Syria was thenceforth ruled in fact by Demetrius' Cretan mercenaries. Again Syria rebelled. Alexander's son, Antiochus (VI), was in the hands of a former minister, Tryphon, who proclaimed his hostage king and set up a rival court in Antioch. At first he was supported by Judaea.

143 B.C.   *The rule of Tryphon in middle Syria*

To curry favor with the Syrian Greeks, Tryphon betrayed and killed Jonathan, the ethnarch of Judaea. According to rumor, he murdered Cleopatra's son also. However that may be, on the death of the boy he proclaimed himself king of Syria.

140 B.C.   *The personal reign of Demetrius II*

Two sons and a daughter had been borne him by Cleopatra. Although Tryphon was well entrenched in middle Syria, the rebel could not extend his domain further without the support of Judaea. Demetrius therefore planned an invasion of Parthia in order to replenish his army and treasury.

Justin XXXVIII, 9: *After invading Parthia . . . and winning several battles he was encircled treacherously, lost his army, and was captured.* [For Justin's account of Demetrius' captivity and marriage to Rodogune, see Introduction to this volume.] After the death of Arsacides, tired of captivity and his obscure though sumptuous existence, Demetrius plotted an escape . . . . He was recaptured by Phraates (II) and guarded more closely, until his Parthian bride gave him children . . . . Phraates then relaxing the guard, Demetrius fled again, was recaptured again. . . . Thereafter he was treated by Phraates gently still, but with contempt . . . .

[The supposed love of Demetrius for Rodogune is either a popular myth or an invention of Appian's. The sequel proves that the assassination of Demetrius did not arise from the Parthian misadventure or marriage.] The news of Demetrius' defeat strengthened Tryphon, who pushed so far into the north that Cleopatra's counselors advised surrender. Antiochus Sidetes, Demetrius' brother, proclaimed himself king.

138 B.C.   *The reign of Antiochus VII Sidetes*

Cleopatra married her brother-in-law, who soon defeated Tryphon and had him executed. One of the five children born of this marriage survived to contest the Seleucid succession.

130 B.C.   *The campaign of Antiochus against Parthia*

Justin XXXVIII, 9: The Parthian clemency toward Demetrius arose neither from the spirit of mercy nor from the marriage connection. *Desiring to conquer Syria, they intended using Demetrius against his brother Antiochus* . . . . [Therefore, Cleopatra had still to fear a Parthian conquest and deposition in favor of Rodogune, but not as a consequence of Demetrius' desires.] Justin XXXVIII, 10: Warned of his danger, Antiochus invaded Parthia. *Phraates then dispatched Demetrius into Syria with a troop of Parthians to regain his throne.*

[Compare *Rodogune*, lines 249–52. But Rodogune could not have accompanied Nicanor into dangers so great.]

129 B.C.   *The death of Antiochus VII*

Caught unprepared by Phraates at the end of winter, Antiochus' army melted and he himself died on the field after falling into the legendary Parthian trap. [Corneille granted his Antiochus a hero's death, but the second detail is transferred to Nicanor (lines 27–28).] A son of Antiochus and a daughter of Demetrius were captured with the remnants of the Syrian army. Demetrius' daughter was taken into Phraates' harem. [According to Riddle this is the source of the imprisonment of Rodogune by Cleopatra. But see below.] Phraates regretted having freed Demetrius and planned an invasion of Syria, from which he was diverted by a revolt of his Scythian mercenaries.

128 B.C.   *The second reign of Demetrius II*

Justin XXXIX, 1: Demetrius was again on his throne, and seeing all Syria mourn the destruction of its army, he resolved to invade Egypt, as if his Parthian adventure and his brother's had ended in success rather than in captivity and death . . . and the Antiochans rebelled. *They execrated the king for his arrogant character that living among the cruel Parthians had rendered intolerable.*

[The last sentence is perhaps echoed by Corneille in Nicanor's violent and spiteful behavior toward Cleopatra and in Rodogune's cruelty to her suitors.]

126 B.C.   *The death of Demetrius II*

Bouché-Leclercq speculates that after the return to Syria Demetrius and Cleopatra lived apart, but he offers no evidence. The crown prince and his brother have at any rate been brought home from Athens, where they had been sent for their education as well as for safety. It is clear that Demetrius' ill-advised Egyptian venture infuriated Cleopatra. He was forced to turn back by the rebellion in Antioch and found the whole country against him, including a new would-be usurper, supported by Ptolemy VII, Alexander Zabinas.

> Justin XXXIX, 1: Defeated, Demetrius was abandoned even by his wife and children. With a few slaves he managed to reach Tyre, intending to take sanctuary in the temple. But the commandant of the city had him slain as he disembarked.

[Was it an oversight on Corneille's part to attribute to Justin the notion that this man was in the pay of Alexander Zabinas? For many and cogent reasons, modern historians, like the ancient world generally, believe that the commandant was acting on Cleopatra's orders. It is probable that Corneille in 1647 attempted to set Justin at loggerheads with other ancient writers, where Justin is not in contradiction but merely vague, in order to divert attention from the extent of his debt. However that may be, there is in Justin no hint that Demetrius' sons had the slightest wish to avenge their calamitous and dangerous father.]

126 B.C.   *The death of Seleucus*

[Justin's account of this event is quoted in the Introduction above. Here and for the death of Cleopatra only dates and comment are given.]

125 B.C.   *The joint reign of Cleopatra Thea and Antiochus VIII Grypus*

The mother may have reigned alone briefly, but the Syrians rebelled, as during Demetrius' captivity, against the sole rule of an Egyptian.

Cleopatra's uncle Ptolemy VII, as her father had done, at first pushed forward the claims of a usurper (Alexander Zabinas) against the true heir to the Syrian crown and then transferred his support and gave a daughter as wife to the latter. The future queen of Syria was the daughter also of Ptolemy's niece-wife, Cleopatra Kokke, to whom he bequeathed the power to crown her favorite son as his successor. [As L. Riddle proposed in *The Genesis and Sources of P. Corneille's Tragedies from "Médée" to "Pertharite"* (Baltimore, 1926), this incident may have suggested to Corneille the similar power enjoyed by Cleopatra Thea in the play.]

121 B.C.   *The reign of Antiochus VIII*

With the help of Ptolemy, Antiochus had defeated Alexander Zabinas (123 B.C.), but not long after Cleopatra's demise, what was to be an endless civil war began between the king and his half-brother, Antiochus Cyzicenus, who accused Grypus of trying to poison him and therefore claimed the throne. As the son of the popular and able Antiochus VII Sidetes, he won the support of all those Syrians, and there were many, who were dismayed by Grypus' improvidence and his taste for composing decadent verse about poisonous snakes. The rivalry of the brothers was in a few years doubled by that of their Egyptian wives, whose ferocity surpassed that of the men.

113 b.c. *The marriage of Cleopatra IV to Cyzicenus*

Cleopatra IV, Tryphaena's older sister, had been divorced by her husband-brother, Ptolemy VIII. To take revenge on all her relations she came to Syria to wed Cyzicenus; and to bring him more than herself alone,

Justin XXXIX, 3: . . . she led as dowry an army seduced from the service of Grypus. [It was probably part of the army of her brother, Cleopatra Kokke's favorite son, whom she had been able to make only ruler of Cyprus. The error in Justin may be that of a scribe.] Thus strengthened, he [Cyzicenus] wages war on his brother.

112 b.c. *The death of Cleopatra IV*

Vanquished, Cyzicenus fled to the city of Antioch. The armies of Grypus followed and laid siege to the city, which sheltered Cleopatra IV also.

Justin XXXIX, 3: When he had captured the city, Grypus's wife commanded that before all else, her sister be found, *not to help her in her captivity, but to see to it that she not escape any of the evils, for she had invaded the kingdom especially to rival herself* [this is of course the source of Rodogune's imprisonment and torture at the hands of Cleopatra Thea], and had become her enemy by marrying the enemy of her husband. *She accused her of bringing foreign forces into a contest of brothers* . . . . *Grypus argued against her, begging that she not force him to commit a deed so foul: women had never suffered at the hands of his ancestors after a victory . . . for they were exempt by their sex from the dangers of war and the rage of the victors.* In this case, one might plead, in addition to the laws of war, the requirements of blood . . . . [Appeals to the voice of nature and the like are dramatic commonplaces. It is Antiochus the conciliator that Corneille found here, as well as the rhythm of certain scenes.] *Every refusal of Grypus aroused further in the sister [Tryphaena] the stubbornness of her sex, who, attributing them not to the spirit of mercy but to love, called soldiers herself and ordered them to spear her sister to death.* [Tryphaena here prefigures Corneille's Cleopatra, whereas in the scene of Cleopatra's death, she had prefigured Rodogune herself. The scene is echoed also in the manner Corneille's Cleopatra takes vengeance into her own hands when her sons reject her commands.] They entered the temple, but unable to tear her away, so strong was her embrace of the image of the goddess, they cut off her hands. Cleopatra [IV] died, cursing the parricides.

111 B.C.   *The death of Cleopatra Tryphaena*

Not long after, there was a second battle, and this time Cyzicenus was victorious. He captured Tryphaena and made of her execution a sacrifice to the spirit of his dead wife. The sons of the two Antiochi inherited lands that had fallen into almost complete anarchy, and the end of the Seleucid dynasty came in less than two decades.

The foregoing contains many seemingly useless details in order to suggest two aspects of the composition of *Rodogune*: first, the extent to which the symmetries and formal regularities of the play are a feature of Justin's history. All commentators have noted the "endlessly repeated atrocities" and the "tedious cycle" in which the Seleucid dynasty runs down to its wretched end. Second, the detailed résumé makes it possible to study precisely how Corneille altered his sources to ennoble every figure, including that of Cleopatra herself. In her context, Cleopatra Thea is much less admirable, but much more understandable, than she is in the play. Indeed, she is almost sympathetic, compared with Demetrius II, her uncle Ptolemy VII, or her daughter-in-law, Tryphaena. The grandeur of Corneille's heroine is paradoxically more imposing as every circumstance that might attenuate her guilt even slightly is removed one by one.

One of the greatest tragedies in the French baroque style, *Rodogune* (first performed late in 1644 or early in 1645) was composed when Corneille was at the peak of his life and career. At once a domestic, historical, political, and psychological tragedy, it has arresting significance for today's world: in portraying the decay of an empire and the erosion of social, religious, and moral values Corneille explores the structure of personal interactions under deep stress.

This volume presents a newly edited French text and a facing-page English prose translation. The introduction, which includes a sketch of the dramatist's career and a critical study of his dramaturgical methods, examines intensively Corneille's sources and suggests a new interpretation of his own account of his inspiration and method of composition. The translator-editor also offers a survey of the criticism of *Rodogune*, which always has been a moot play, and argues that Corneille's estimate of this work, which he set above *Le Cid* and *Polyeucte*, is more than authorial partiality: in beauty of conception, power of movement, and brilliance of construction, it equals his finest works, while in its fusion of violence with psychological subtlety it surpasses them.